William S. Burroughs with Kiki at the Café Central, Socco Chico, Tangiers, 1954.

LETTERS TO ALLEN GINSBERG
1953-1957

William Burroughs

Full Court Press

NEW YORK

Copyright © 1982 by William Burroughs.
Introduction copyright © 1981 by Allen Ginsberg.
All rights reserved.

Letters to Allen Ginsberg appeared in a limited, bilingual edition from
Editions Claude Givaudan/Am Here Books, Geneva, 1978.

Library of Congress Cataloging in Publication Data

Burroughs, William S., 1914–
  Letters to Allen Ginsberg, 1953-1957.

  Includes index.
  1. Burroughs, Willism S., 1914– —Correspondence.
2. Ginsberg, Allen, 1926—Correspondence. 3. Authors,
American—20th century—Correspondence. I. Ginsberg,
Allen, 1926–   II. Title.
PS3552.U75Z49   813'.54 [B]   81-22109
ISBN 0-916190-16-1   AACR2
ISBN 0-916190-17-X (pbk.)

Photos from the Allen Ginsberg archive at Butler Library, Columbia University, printed by Marty Messik.

Printed in the United States of America by Capital City Press, Montpelier, Vermont. Typesetting by Unitron
Graphics, New York. Second printing .

Full Court Press
138-140 Watts Street
New York, N.Y. 10013

EDITORS' NOTES: The editors wish to thank the following for their help in the preparation of this edition: Allen Ginsberg, Bob Rosenthal, James Grauerholz, Richard Aaron, and the staff of the Special Collections, Butler Library, Columbia University.

Although most of the letters in this volume are to Allen Ginsberg, a few are to Neal Cassady, Jack Kerouac, Louis Ginsberg, and Alan Ansen.

Footnotes throughout are by Allen Ginsberg, except where indicated by brackets. Other editorial additions also appear in brackets.

Ron Padgett and Anne Waldman

Contents

  1 *Un Homme de Lettres. Un Poème Moderne.*
       Preface by William Burroughs
  5 *Recollections of Burroughs Letters*
       by Allen Ginsberg
 11 *The Letters*
199 *Index*

UN HOMME DE LETTRES. UN POÈME MODERNE.

Leafing through these letters gives me a ghostly sensation of being called upon to comment on someone else's old literary letters, a cardboard box of yellowed and mildewed correspondence tucked away in an attic by a former landlady, the ancient saga of a moaning man of letters: complaints about food, service, accomodations, poor health and lack of money—(As a matter of fact his financial difficulties are exaggerated, as he was fortunate to have an allowance of $200 per month from his parents, quite enough to live comfortably in Tangiers at that time. The same goes for his complaints of ill health, since he was blessed with an exceedingly strong constitution). His publishers, who are cheating him; his rejection by the foreign colony, which he characterizes as beneath his notice; his hopes of getting what he really means down on paper, and his despair of ever doing so.

How familiar it all seems. So many others sigh from these yellowed pages, the same querulous voice: "On top of all this I have a terrible cold" . . . "Why did I ever leave Mexico?" . . . "Fifty dollars to last me until Feb. 1st" . . . "Absolutely no one of the slightest interest in Tangiers, am reduced to the companionship of shoeshine boys" . . . "Ill for the past week. Joints painful and swollen. Light fever. My check unaccountably delayed and I haven't a cent. Living on bread and tea—"

His endless struggle with drugs or alcohol: "Down to 20 mg. per day now" . . . "Still on my regime of one drink a day. Meg and Stan were amazed at my fortitude" . . . "An unfortunate condition of neuralgia in the back—I have never known such pain—has forced my dosage up again" . . . "Terrible row with Zelda has thrown me off my schedule—"

His long-suffering companions; any failure of attendance and he screams out "Sick and broke and now even Kiki has deserted me". He still has the strength for a scurrilous obscene attack on his publishers, in his deep conviction that the world exists to serve him and any failure to do so evidences the rankest ingratitude and treachery.

His inability to sit down and write a novel: "It's all in bits and pieces, like spores taking root and growing anywhere . . . the talking asshole, the junk infusions he gives President Eisenhower, it's never quite *right* somehow and I had to hock my typewriter for junk money. This is Friday night. *No check at the Embassy.* I must have turned quite grey, because the doorman stepped forward to steady me—'Are you all right Mr. Burroughs?' I explained to him that I had just received some *terrible news.* I could only just totter home . . . "

His overextended credit at the drug stores of Tangiers, where he is a well-known figure, always neatly dressed and polite . . . One courtly old Spanish druggist hailed him as a real gentleman, a *caballero.* Living on brown sugar and fruit, reclaiming his typewriter, he complains that he is badly received at Dean's Bar.

In *The Road to Xanadu*, John Livingston Lowes traces the sources of Coleridge's poetic imagery in the books that he is known to have read, and shows the conversion of raw material—mostly from accounts of sea voyages—into *The Rhyme of the Ancient Mariner* and other poems. These letters to Allen Ginsberg present a devious road to *Naked Lunch* from the raw material of junk experience, as set forth in *Junky* and in these letters. Despite the writer's subsequent claims that junk is absolutely contraindicated for creative writing, and that *Naked Lunch* could not have been written unless he had gotten off junk, one is amazed to discover that a great deal of *Naked Lunch was actually written* in these letters to Allen Ginsberg, at a time when the writer was often heavily addicted and at no time free from addiction. It would seem that opiates do not extinguish creativity, but that after a certain point they do fail to nourish it. One is forcefully reminded of de Quincey's *Confessions of an English Opium Eater*, where he describes the gloom, the oppression and feeling of death, brought on by heavy overdosage: "like I was buried in a stone coffin in Neolithic mud". However, reduction of dosage leads to an almost miraculous restoration of health and good spirits.

The experience of drugs, like all experience, is transmuted by the writer into what we call art. In these letters we see this transmutation of experience as it occurs, dated and in context. I have often thought that writers do not write; they read what is already written and transcribe. So perhaps they are not complaining about ill health, lack of money, and rejection, but about the bondage of a calling that keeps them laboriously transcribing cryptic messages in rapidly disappearing ink, like the traces of a dream, year after year . . . "It eluded us then; tomorrow we will run faster, stretch out our arms further, and one fine morning—So we beat on, boats against the current, borne back ceaselessly into the past".

"Cashier's check preferable if not too much trouble—"
"Kiki back on the job—"
"Address Cargo U.S. Consulate, Tangiers—"
"The Embassy has moved to Rabat—"
"P.S. My illness blew over for the present. But it will be back—I can feel it lurking about—"
"Write me 202 Sanford Avenue, Palm Beach, Florida—"

Un homme de lettres. Un poème moderne.

Recollections of Burroughs Letters
By Allen Ginsberg

I adore the writer of these letters full of black humor and suffering querulousness. Kerouac at this time called Burroughs "the most intelligent man in America" and decades later I'd say he was right. At least I can't think of anyone more basically to the point. "Genius is funny," Kerouac also said, thinking Shakespeare. I burst out laughing 25 years later, reading Burroughs' directions to Seymour Wyse where to "find the action" (letter May 30, 1956).

But a few paragraphs on the circumstances of these letters might be useful. We'd known each other since 1945, we lived together for a few months 1953 in idyllic pre-Viet-war Lower East Side between Avenues B & C on East 7th Street, visited by Kerouac, Corso and other friends, had assembled the text of *Yage Letters* & *Queer* &'d had a love affair. In the end, despite my admiration and affection for my teacher, I had rejected his body. "I don't want your ugly old cock." Harsh words for a young man, something I wouldn't want anyone to say to me. But he had pushed me to it, after long ambivalence, by offering, nay, threatening to "schlupp" with me, i.e. devour my soul parasitically, as Bradley the Buyer does to the District Supervisor in *Naked Lunch*. This word was part of an exquisite black-humorous fantasy on Bill B.'s part, hardly the thing to woo a scared lad (I was bodily ungainly anyway), and a parody of his feelings, lest his desire be considered offensive. So he wooed with extravagant self-deprecatory suggestiveness. It scared me, the responsibility to be his love connection. Unlimited sensitivity and vulnerability, I understood at the time, and respected, idolized. Not sure if some monstrous Crab Nebula ambassador was not behind his implacable love, I reacted with naive impatience one afternoon on the NE corner of E. 7th Street and Avenue B, "I don't want . . .", affronting his trust boorishly, in rude panic—I ever regret the wound I dealt his heart.

We decided to separate for a season. We'd been spiritual-literary friends since Kerouac and I had decided to visit him in 1945 to pay our respects and inquire after his soul. Among close friends, *Junky, Yage Letters, Pull My Daisy, The Green Automobile, The First Third, On the Road, Visions of Cody, Subterreaneans* had already been written and "published in heaven" if not on earth—we stayed still faithful to the star on each other's forehead, still sacramental life-companions despite disturbance of erotic rapport. I loved Bill and he loved me, as I still do decades later. Wouldn't you?

So he sailed to Europe, eventually Tangier, and I hitchhiked to visit his earlier boyfriend Marker in Jacksonville, then spent Xmas with Burroughs' parents living in Palm Beach, stayed in Yucatan and Chiapas half a year, then trained to San Jose in the Bay Area near San Francisco to meet Neal Cassady (with whom I was erotically enamored as much as Bill was heart-aching for me) and Kerouac.

In this context of trust, love and heartache we continued a correspondence already years old (*Junky* and *Yage Letters* already were composed from his half the previous three years' epistles). The reader will thus recognize many of the "routines", that later became *Naked Lunch*, as conscious projections of Burroughs' love fantasies—further explanations and parodies and models of our ideal love schlupp together.

I was somewhat resistant, so much of his fantasy consists of a parody of his invasion of my body and brain. At the time I was experimenting with heterosexual amity and was shacked up with a fellow worker girl in the market research and advertising world of Nob Hill and smart San

Francisco Montgomery Street. This appeared as a terrible affront to Bill's hope of marriage of heart and soul with me; I was just trying out my capacity for love of all kinds and accommodation to Commercial Society. I made direct heart exchange with Peter Orlovsky within a year.

The bulk of letters written to S.F. from Tangier are Bill's faithful record of his heroic battle with depression and junk, Burroughs transcending his own condition to examine World Condition, prophesying and articulating a Post-Nuclear psychology. (See letter Jan. 12, 1955 "under the spreading black cloud a final bomb.") Exploring his own soul, till he reached the bottom, he emptied his soul out and entered at last the open blue space of "Benevolent indifferent attentiveness" characteristic of later phases of his art.

These letters are a record of Burroughs' suffering from a "Dark Night of the Soul", the necessary experience of recognition and purification, or clearing out, of love-wounded fantasy. A chronicle of Burroughs at his most vulnerable, "the invisible man" at his most visible tender, in a self-humbling open-hearted phase, longing and desirous, offering body and inmost self-regard for inspection and acceptance. A tremendous sweetness and willingness comes through, as in the letter to Jack Aug. 18, 1954 and one to myself May 17, 1955—"I am having Serious difficulties with my novel. I tell you the novel form is Completely inadequate to express what I have to say. I don't know if I can find a form. I am very gloomy as to the prospects of publication. And I'm not like you, Jack, I need an audience, of course, a small audience. But I still need publication for development . . ." "Wish you were here as I could do with some outside help."

I was inadequate to answer this weight of love—not smart enough to be the object on which he lavished such inventive genius—not openhearted enough to give him what he needed, wanted, and deserved—a dearer answer than I gave. I felt ashamed of my own shallowness. My own letters in return for his have not survived, I'm almost glad, they'd show the poverty of my own art and superficial appreciation of his attentive devotion to me. His letters go through phases of suit and rejection, somewhat similar in structure to Shakespeare's sonnet sequence to his boyfriend Mr. W.H.. First evidence of cut-up is displayed as reunion between us approaches, after 4 years. Here Burroughs the letter writer person (Jan. 31, 1957) nearly merges with the routines that pass before his eyes. The letters merge with the novel, the life merges with the art. He has won through, become one with his imagination, and begins to assume gigantic solitary proportions as Artist alone in the universe, somewhat mysterious, somewhat dehumanized behind mask of Artist, more aloof, and later more outrageous than ever. By 1961, our next reunion in Tangier, he was a hash-eating rambunctious machete-swinging holy laughing terror, cutting up his prose and "all apparent sensory phenomena."

Alas! the most extravagant passages, abject letters of complete schlupp-longing, and prophetic curse at my ingratitude, have been censored by the author. A red heart valentine center has been removed—the elder distinguished Mr. B. of the preface to this volume has judged himself (and me?) too harshly and excised some evidence of sentimental romance from this collection as edited and printed here—lines blue-penciled in various letters, a few pages irrevocably burnt.

Despite emendations, Burroughs' presentations of these epistolary confessions is an act of benevolence. They are revealing, personal, wild, sensitive, foolish, sublime, sweet and self-deceiving, frank and soft. How can he stand such a self-portrait, so many decades later? Yet he's given himself away—the strange Burroughs that Kerouac and I knew, the gentle Melancholy Blue Boy, the proud elegant sissy, the old charmer, the intelligent dear. I kept his letters, snapshots, envelopes in black springboard binders; the text of *Naked Lunch* ("an endless novel which will drive everybody mad") accumulated till 1957 when I was free to join Bill and Kerouac in Tangier. Jack lived two floors above Bill's at the Villa Mouniria in a balcony room overlooking the Straits of Gibralter. He had begun retyping the preliminary assemblage of texts and letters which compose *Naked Lunch*. I was to bring my entire text mss.—hundreds of pages, in chronological order of invention, to Tangier. There all of us were to sit together and assemble a final manuscript. The difficulty was that Dr. Benway and other characters introduced from 1953 on were refined and developed from letter to letter with new adventures and routines and additional skits and episodes. How to weave it all together? My idea was to present it chronologically, so that the theme or plot would be the actual development, in time, of the ideas as they changed through 3-4 years, visible to the reader, one superimposed on another, developing and integrating with each other, as they did in the letters, accounting B.'s changes of psyche, and extension of fantasy—the mad doctor in his operating room superimposed on purple-assed baboon motorcyclist superimposed on Roosevelt's cabinet massacres invented earlier in N.Y. '53.

The problem of compositional structure was never resolved that season—Kerouac completed one section of typing, I began retyping another, separating personal-letter matter from imaginative improvisation and fantasy and "routine" matter. Alan Ansen arrived, and with more powerful typist genius took on the greater burden of preparing the mss. So when it was time after several months—half a year?—for me and Peter to leave on our first visit of Europe, I entrusted the two springboard binders to Ansen, who in his apartment of those years in Venice and later in Athens housed a rare collection of mss., incunabula—Auden's letters and drafts of *Age of Anxiety*, correspondence with Thomas Mann on Wagner's prosody.

The final editing arrangement of *Naked Lunch* in Paris two years later was a dramatic accident. Sinclair Beiles, Burroughs' friend working with Olympia Press, said that Maurice Girodias wanted to publish the entire book on the basis of his reading of sections prepared for Chicago's

Big Table magazine. Girodias' message was that the manuscript had to be ready for printer in two weeks. By Burroughs' account: "We worked away, sending pieces to the printer as soon as they were typed up. When we got proofs back Beiles said, 'I don't think anything needs to be done at all.' The way it came off the typewriter was the way it worked. I looked at it and said, 'I think you're right.' Only one change was made—the placement of the first passage on the detectives (Hauser and O'Brien) shifted toward the end. From the time that Girodias sent Sinclair over saying I want to publish the novel to its printing was only one month."

At the time I was proud, pleased and inspired to receive the letters, which were shared with Neal and Jack and Philip Whalen and Gary Snyder and Robert Creeley.° If nothing else of my own history survives, I'd be happily remembered as the sympathetic kid to whom W.S. Burroughs addressed his tender intelligence in these letters containing major sketches of *Naked Lunch*. This is the heart of the man behind *Naked Lunch*, and the years of its creation—a classic example of struggling artist—and inspiration for all writers working in the vast solitude of Art.

The literary-historical record will be filled out by reference to *As Ever* and *Straight Hearts Delight*, contemporary letters (circa 1953-60) between Neal Cassady and self, and Peter and self. Publication of correspondence with Kerouac and Corso will give ampler realistic picture of those decades' thoughts and unconditional friendship.

New York, February-April 1981

°The Interzone City Market Meet Cafe passage was published by Creeley in 1957 *Black Mt. Review* 7, the first Burroughs prose (since *Junky*, 1952) related to *Naked Lunch* and subsequent grand style to be printed in America.

Left to right: Allen Ginsberg, William Burroughs, and Gregory Corso, Villa Mouniria, Tangier, 1961.

1.
Dec. 21, 53
Rome

Dear Allen,

In all my experience as a traveller I have never encountered anything to compare with that lousy Greek ship. Long greasy hairs in the jam, dirty glasses, dirty dishes, dirty staterooms, uneatable food, non-existent service, and 12 days.

Arriving in Rome I find neither Ansen nor any word from him. Letter from Kells. He will meet me later in Tangers.) Rome is expensive and cold, and seemingly offers nothing for a man of my caliber. (Expecting Ansen to be here with his address book in accordance with our arrangement, I brought along no addresses. Can't find the baths anywhere. I have visited every bath in the phone book. Can't find anything that offers any interest.) I plan to leave here in the next few days and proceed to Africa. This Rome detour is costing me over $100, incalculable inconvenience and boredom.

I wish I had come to Mexico with you.

Hope you are faring better. I received your letter for which many thanks.

As ever,
Bill

P.S. On top of it all I have a terrible cold and prospect of 24 hours on 3rd class train from here to Gibraltar (24 hours is wishful thinking—48 more like.).

Kells Elvins: Harvard schoolmate of Bill's—with Burroughs, co-author of *The Twilight's Last Gleaming*, an early skit on ship *Titanic* sinking, AKA *So Proudly We Hail*.

2.
Dec 24, '53
Rome

Dear Allen,

Alan is showing tonight.

As for Rome. In all my experience as a traveller I never see a more miserable place. I would rather be in Bogota —yes even in Quito.

Finally found the baths. They have been closed. In all this town is no Turkish bath. Now you would think there would be bars like the San Remo etc., but such is not the case. I live in the Latin quarter, and I have ransacked this town. Properly speaking there are no bars in Rome. A Roman "bar" is a hole in the wall soda and ice cream joint, no toilet and no place to sit down, with the door propped open or missing altogether, where you can gulp a drink with a cold, blue hand. It's cold here like N.Y. in Winter and you *never get warm.* There's no heat anywhere. *And* Rome is considerably more expensive than N.Y. Right now I am huddled in my room (wearing overcoat, of course. You never take off your overcoat in Rome.) With a terrible cold, reading *The Invisible Man*.

I plan to leave here the 28th and straight to Tangers. Glad Kells did not come here on my account.

Love,
Bill

The hottest spot in Rome looks like that coffee joint I don't like next to the Remo (Rienzi's??). Some picture on the wall showing a bleak lack of talent, a few dreary dykes in sweat shirts, a sprinkle of ugly queers, and some characters with beards playing chess. A real cute waiter named "Chi Chi." However, since he is the son of the owner it looks like hands off.

Why did I ever leave Mexico?

3.
Jan. 2, '54
Rome
Saturday

Dear Allen,

Leaving Monday for Tanger via Gibraltar. Will arrive wth $50 to last me until Feb. 1st.

The more I see of Rome the less I like it. Considerably more expensive than N.Y.C., cold like you never get warm because there is virtually no heat. No interest in this town at all. I have made some contacts, and confirmed my impression that Rome was in a clean–up campaign. The Turkish baths have been closed. The heat is on junk, and the junkies of Rome are shivering sick in their traps. Alan was on the point of renting an apartment, but the landlord flipped when he heard I was going to flop on the couch for three days. So the deal fell through. Did you ever hear the like of that? Anyone comes in your trap even for *one night* has to be registered with the law. Colombia was freedom hall compared with this dump. And under no circumstances no matter how respectable can you have anyone who is not registered in the hotel up for a drink. Not for *10 minutes*. I am going to have something to say to Gore Vidal, and all these characters talking about how great Italy is and anything goes, and they got like a renaissance of culture. What a crock of shit! They can shove Italy all the way up. And incidentally I hear France is no better and twice as expensive. I am beginning to think there is no place like Mexico, and I wish to God I had gone with you to California. Well I will dig North Africa. Alan has been a little bit more happy here since he goes for cathedrals and such, and can stand cold weather. Also he has negotiated several *affairs de coeur* in frigid doorways (average price $10 and pretty shoddy merchandise).

Let me hear from you. Alan sends buckets of love.

As ever,
Love,
Bill

Dear Allen,

No the price is only $3.20, but there may be extras if you suck in a buggy instead of a doorway. The fountains are wonderful (even old Cactus Boy melted at the sight of Trevi), and I feel that in spite of minor irritations Europe is just wonderful. Enjoy Yucatán and give my love to Neal.

                Love,
                    Alan (Ansen)

P.S. After this why I can never see a drugstore the same way again. Paregoric *is*, really, rather yummy.

                4.
            Jan. 20, 1954
              Tanger

Dear Allen,

Driving down to Casablanca in a few days with an enigmatic Englishman (Import-Export line) to see if I can find a job there. If not, back here for a few months in any case. Tanger is cheap but higher than Mexico. Plenty boys, but I got no place to take one (the hotel is strictly respectable.) Poor grade of tea. P.G. in the drug stores.

The most loathsome types produced by the land of the free are represented in the American Colony of Tanger. There are like 2 American bars. No. 1 I hit dead cold sober at 1 o'clock on a Sunday afternoon. Horrible vista of loud-mouthed, red-faced drunks, falling off bar stools, puking in corners, a Céline nightmare. Bar No. 2 is stocked with the dreariest breed of piss elegant, cagy, queens (Blue Parrot timber). For example some rich old fuck has in tow a horrible looking, tired, pretentious, big toothed, sallow-faced young fruit so he comes in this joint to show off the fine thing he latched onto. The payoff is in struts a great blond beast of a non-queer Marine captain (impeccably dressed in pinstripe suit), insulting and flirtatious, battening on the idiotic adulation of decaying queens. I figured I'd had it at that point so paid an exorbitant bill and left.

Nowadays I spend my time smoking weed with shoeshine boys in Arab cafés. Their manners are better and their conversation quite as interesting.

O has folded and the editor is in Mexico. Bowles is in New York. All in all I still say Mexico is *the* place, but since I am here will give it a thorough trial. So far I don't meet any writers or anybody of interest. Like I say, reduced to the companionship of shoeshine boys. Well let me hear from you.

As ever,
Bill

[Struts: walking style.]
[*O: Zero*, the magazine.]

5.
Jan. 26 [1954]
Tanger

Dear Allen,

I like Tanger less all the time. No writers colony here or they keep themselves hid some place. Everybody has both feet in your business; like some character I never see before says: "Your friend Ali is in the Socco Chico. Please give me one peseta." And the payoff is I never get to lay Ali. No place to take him. You can't check into a cheap hotel here like in a civilized country. No they want inflated whorehouse prices when they see what the score is. And Ali is getting worried about his standing in the shoeshine set (he is afraid some one might think I am scr°°°°g/careful about obscenity in the mails/him). He thumps his little scrawny chest and says "I am a man". Oh God! Such shit I could hear in Clayton Mo. Their lousy weed tears your throat out like it's cut with horse shit. And no more boot than corn silk. I try to connect for some O, and a citizen sells me some old dried up poppy pods. Well I will have a good look around since I am here. May change my mind. Would God I was back in Mexico. Or Peru.

What's all this old Moslem culture shit? One thing I have learned. I know what Arabs do all day and all night. They sit around smoking cut weed and playing some silly card game. And don't ever fall for this inscrutable oriental shit like Bowles puts down. They are just a gabby, gossipy, simple minded, lazy crew of citizens.

[Remainder of letter missing.]

6.
Feb. 1, 1954
Tanger

Dear Allen,

Cold here like the Penal Colony. I feel like I just lost my last connection. In fact I did just lose one or at any rate the bastard didn't show today, and me half hooked as usual. Seems like no white stuff here. Just gum and not much of that.

I got drunk the other night at a get-together of the ultra chic American Colony. For all I know groped the British Chargé-d'affaires or some other dignitary. On the wagon again.

They have an arrangement here I never saw elsewhere in all my experience as a traveller: Private Turkish bath cubicles *"à deux"*. 60 ¢. This solves the hotel problem. But the boys got like a union. They all expect $5. And a pretty crummy lot they are too. I never see such abject, repulsive, whining panhandling. A man might contract some loathsome venereal disease of the soul from these untouchables. Besides which it costs an additional $3 in Aureomycin for adequate pro coverage fore and aft.

There is no writer colony here. I have met no one of the slightest interest in Tanger.

[Remainder of letter missing.]
The Penal Colony: Kafka's story was on our minds.

7.
Feb. 7, 1954
Tanger

Dear Allen,

Here is my latest attempt to write something saleable. All day I had been finding pretexts to avoid work, reading magazines, making fudge, cleaning my shot-gun, washing the dishes, going to bed with Kiki, tying the garbage up in neat parcels and putting it out for the collector—(if you put it out in a waste basket or any container they will steal the container every time. I was going to chain a basket to my doorstep but it's like too much trouble. So I put it out in packages—buying food for dinner, picking up a junk script. So finally I say: "Now you must work" and smoke some tea and sit down and out it comes all in one piece like a glob of spit: "The incredibly obscene, thinly disguised references and situations that slip by in Grade B movies, the double entendres, perversion, sadism of popular songs, poltergeist knockings and mutterings of America's putrifying unconscious, boils that swell until they burst with a fart noise as if the body had put out an auxilary ass hole with a stupid, belligerent Bronx cheer.

"Did I ever tell you about the man who taught his ass hole to talk? His whole abdomen would move up and down, you dig, farting out the words. It was unlike anything I ever heard (being a decent girl and don't you forget it, Mister.). 'Some people think just because they take a girl to dinner at Dysentery Dave's Ox Ball House, they can go and get physical.' 'This is Jaundice Johnny's Second Run V. (Viscera) Room, my dear—' (I am cutting a long portion on second-run reject liver that doesn't pass the inspector because of live worms etc. A whole section on parasitic worms.)

"This ass talk had a sort of gut frequency. It hit you right down there like you gotta go. You know when the old colon gives you the elbow and it feels sorta cold inside, and you know all you have to do is turn loose? Well this talking hit you right down there, a bubbly, thick, stagnate sound, a sound you could *smell*.

"This man worked for a carnival, you dig, and to start with it was like a novelty ventriloquist act. Real funny, too—at first. He had a number he called 'The Better Olé' that was a scream, I tell you. I forget most of it but it was clever like 'Oh I say, are you still down there old thing?' 'Nah! I had to go relieve myself.'

"After a while the ass started talking on its own. He would go in without anything prepared and his ass would ad lib and toss the gags back at him every time.

"Then it developed sort of teeth, like little raspy incurving hooks, and started eating. He thought this was cute at first and built an act around it, but the ass hole would eat its way through his pants and start talking on the street, shouting out it wanted equal rights. It would get drunk too, and have crying jags nobody loved it and it wanted to be kissed same as any other mouth. Finally it talked all the time day and night, you could hear him for blocks screaming at it to shut up, and beating it with his fist, and sticking candles up it, but nothing did any good and the ass hole said to him: 'It's you who will shut up in the end. Not me. Because we don't need you around here anymore. I can talk and eat *and* shit.'

"After that he began waking up in the morning with a transparent jelly like a tadpole's tail all over his mouth. This jelly was what the scientists call Un D.T.— undifferentiated tissue—which could grow into any kind of flesh on the human body. He would tear it off his mouth and the pieces would stick to his hands like burning gasoline jelly and grow there, grow anywhere on him a glob of it fell. So finally his mouth sealed over, and the whole head would have amputated spontaneous (Did you know there is a condition occurs in parts of Africa and only among Negroes where the little toe amputates spontaneously?) —except for the *eyes*, you dig? That's one thing the ass hole *couldn't* do, was see. It needed the eyes. But nerve connections were blocked and infiltrated and atrophied so the brain couldn't give orders any more. It was trapped in the shell, sealed off. For a while you could see the silent, helpless suffering of the brain behind the eyes, then finally the brain must have died, because the eyes went out, there was no more feeling in them than a crab's eye on the end of a stalk.

"So what I started to talk about was the sex that passes the censor, squeezes through *between* bureaus, because there's always a space *between,* in popular songs and Grade B movies, as giving away the basic American rottenness, spurting out like breaking boils, throwing out globs of that Un D.T. to fall anywhere and grow into some degenerate, cancerous life form, reproducing a hideous random image. Some would be entirely made of penis-like erectile tissue, others of viscera barely covered over with skin, clusters of 3 and 4 eyes together, criss cross of mouths and ass holes, human parts shaken around and poured out any way they fall. Result of complete cellular representation is cancer. Democracy is cancerous, and bureaus are its cancer. A bureau takes root anywhere in the state, turns malignant like the Narcotics Bureau, and grows and grows, always reproducing more of its own kind, until it chokes the host if not controlled or excised. Bureaus cannot live without a host, being true parasitic organisms. A Corporation on the other hand *can* live without the state. That is the road to follow. The building up of independent units to meet *needs* of the people who participate in the functioning of the unit. A bureau functions on opposite principle of *inventing needs* to justify its existence, but the *need must always come first*. Bureaucracy is wrong as a cancer, a turning away from the human evolutionary direction of infinite potentials and differentiation and independent, spontaneous action, to the complete parasitism of a virus—(It is thought that the virus is a degeneration from more complex life form. It may at one time have been capable of independent life. Now has fallen to the border line between living and dead matter. It can only exhibit living qualities in a host, by *using the life of another.*)—the renunciation of life itself, *falling* towards unorganic, inflexible machines, towards dead matter. Bureaus die when the structure of the state collapses. They are as helpless and unfit for independent existence as a displaced tape worm or a virus that has killed the host.

"In Timbuctu once I saw an Arab boy who could play the flute with his ass, and the fairies told me he was really an individual in bed. He could play a tune up and down the organ, hitting the most erogenously sensitive spots —which are different on everyone, of course. Every lover had his theme song which was perfect for him and rose to his climax. The boy was a great artist when it came to improvising new combines and special climaxes, some of them notes in the unknown, tie-ups of seeming discords that would suddenly breach through each other, and crush together with a stunning, hot, sweet impact."

This is my saleable product. Do you dig what happens? It's almost like automatic writing produced by a hostile, independent entity who is saying in effect "I will write what I please." At same time when I try to pressure myself into organizing production, to impose some form on material, or even to follow a line (like continuation of novel) the effort catapults me into a sort of madness where only the most extreme material is available to me. What a disaster to lose my typewriter, and no possibility of buying one this month. My financial position slides inexorably. I started off this month in debt and in hock until I absolutely couldn't have promoted another centavo. I am afraid to count—will do that Monday morning—but I think I have $60 left. That's $2 per day for this month. Wouldn't be so bad if I didn't need junk. I spend $2 per day on junk alone. And I give Kiki 50¢ per day pocket money, and I have to feed him. He found work for three weeks, but the job gave out. His mother is sick and she can't work so he has to support her. My 50¢ goes, usually, to his mother. Then he will want another 50¢ to see a football game or a movie. Well enough of all this dreary ledger so inexorably in the red. I found a copy of *Zero*, the magazine put out in Tanger by one Albert Benveniste (Now deceased—*Zero*, I mean, not Albert who may be flourishing for all I know). It's terrible.

I have started writing a Chandler-style straight action story about some super Heroin you can get a habit on one shot with it or something similar—I'm not even sure yet. But it starts out 2 detectives come to arrest me. I know I am to be used in experiments with this drug (They don't know this.). To save myself I kill them both. That is where I am now. On the lam. Waiting to score for ½ ounce of junk to hide out with, the alarm is going out right now; to every prowl car, every precinct, etc. etc. Don't ask me what is going to happen I just don't know. May turn allegorical or even sur - realist. *A ver*.

I read interesting case. England. 2 naval Lieutanants. Good friends. Drinking. One hits a shot glass every time at six feet with his pistol. The other picks up a hat and holds it in his hand, and says "shoot it." The Lieutenant shot a hole in it. Later on the 2nd part puts the hat on his head and says "Now try it." Then, at a distance of six feet, the Lt. in the first part takes *careful aim at the very top of the hat* and fires (there were witnesses) hitting his friend in the head. Friend may live, though.

Do you know the story of Mike Fink? He'd been shooting shot glasses off the bar all afternoon. Finally a young friend of his put a shot glass on his head and Mike missed and killed the boy. The bartender did not believe it was an accident because Mike was known as a good shot. He got his own gun and shot Fink dead. (Another case in Durango, Mexico. Politico in whorehouse tried to shoot glass off whore's head. Killed her.).

By the time it takes for you to receive this letter and answer it, I will be most urgently in need of money (Sorry, just find I already mentioned this.). But please try to send me some. The loss of my typewriter was a real disaster. I don't want to lose my camera. I am going on a budget and will do my best to make it so I don't get in debt again . . .

       Love,
       Bill

P.S. Personal check is O.K. as I know someone here with bank account. Don't bother with those international money orders as they take three weeks to clear. Cashier's check preferable if not too much trouble.

       8.
       Feb. 9, 1954
       Tanger
       Morocco

Dear Allen,

 Waiting for Kells to show. Expect him here momentarily. This town is left over from a boom. Hotels and bars empty. Vast, pink stucco apartment houses falling apart, not even finished. In a few years Arab families will move in with goats and chickens. I have a room in best district for 50¢ per day. You can eat in native quarter for 20¢. But boys and sweet opium keep me broke. You can get a boy for $1 or even less, but the Aureomycin procoverage comes high. I have been doing some writing. Will send along samples when I locate a typewriter.

This town seems to have several dimensions. I have experienced a series of Kafkian incidents that would certainly have sent Carl back to the nut house. For example I go to bed with an Arab in European clothes. Several days later in the rain (and loaded on hash. You eat it here with hot tea.) I meet an Arab in native dress, and we repair to a Turkish bath. Now I am almost (but not quite), sure it is the same Arab. In any case I have not seen no. 1 again. When I walk down the street Arabs I never see before greet me in a manner suggesting unspeakable familiarity (in past or future?). I told one of these Arabs "Look, I don't like you and I don't know you. Scram." He just laughed and said "I see you later, Mister." And I did in fact go to bed with him later, or at least I think it was the same one. It's like I been to bed with 3 Arabs since arrival, but I wonder if it isn't the same character in different clothes, and every time better behaved, cheaper, more respectful (he has learned I can't be pushed beyond a certain point). I *really* don't know for sure. Next time I'll notch one of his ears.

I enclose communication for Hoeniger. I explained to Hoeniger not once but many times that *all* tourist cards are issued by the Consulate. The Consul gives the cards, already signed, to airlines and travel agencies who fill the cards out and sell them to travellers. I checked with Avianca in N.Y. They have the cards already signed by the Consul. I carefully explained this to Hoeniger. Write to me % U.S. Legation, Tanger. My best to Neal.

                        As ever,
                          Love,
                            Bill

P.S.   Paul Bowles is here, but kept in seclusion by an Arab boy who is insanely jealous and given to the practice of black magic. May go down to Dakar. There is a lot of work there.

Hoeniger: Bert Hoeniger, a lawyer friend, classmate of A.G. at Columbia College.

9.
March 1 [1954]
Tanger

Dear Allen,

Tanger is looking up. Meeting the local expatriates. Junkies, queers, drunks, about like Mexico. Most of them came from someplace else for obvious reasons.

Sample Tanger nocturne: Arrive in the Mar Chica, all-night bar where everybody goes after midnight. With me an Irish boy who left England after a spot of trouble, and a Portuguese who can't go home again. Both queer. Both ex-junkies. Both chippying with dollies (script not exactly necessary). Both flat broke. The Portuguese wants me to invest in a pornographic picture enterprise, and also go back in The Business. Proprietor of Mar Chica looks like 1890 ex-prize fighter, a bit fat, but still a man of great strength and exceedingly evil disposition. Beautiful Arab boy behind the bar. Languid animal grace, a bit sulky, charming smile. Every queer in Tanger has propositioned him, but he won't play.

Two Lesbians who work on a smuggling ship drunk at a table. Spanish workmen, queers, British sailors.

Taylor seizes me and drags me to the bar, throwing an arm around my shoulder, and tightening his grip whenever I try to edge away. He gazes into my face, putting down a sincere routine. "Life is rotten here, Bill.

Rotten. It's the end of the world, Tanger. Don't you feel it, Bill? You've got to have some ideal, something to hang onto—where do you live, Bill?"

"Oh, oh near the Place de France."

"Bill, you understand about money? What can I *do* Bill? Tell me. I'm disgusted." He clutches my arm. "I'm scared, Bill. Scared of the future, scared of life. You understand." He seems on the point of climbing in my lap like a child, convulsed by a hideous hunger for absolution.

I disengage myself and sit down with the two Lesbians and the Irish boy. One of the Lesbians looks at me blearily like a Third Avenue Irish drunk.

"What does *fuck you* mean?"

"I don't know."

"Well fuck you anyway." She begins to cry and clutch the other Lesbian. "My child, my poor child. You're such an old drab."

Like you see Tanger is almost too pat. No lower age limit on boys. An American I know keeps a 13-year-old kid—"If they can walk I don't want them." Trouble is the Arabs are an awful looking people.

I am hooked. Met a doctor's son, he need money, and the old man's script pad right there. Some stuff called Eukodol which is best junk kick I ever had. Start dolly cure in a few days now.

They got vicious, purple-assed baboons in the mountains a few miles out of town (Paul Bowles was set upon by enraged baboons and forced to flee for his life). I intend to organize baboon sticks from motorcycles. A sport geared to modern times.

Have done some work, but I feel dissatisfied with it. I have to find a completely new approach. Wasting too much time sitting around in cafés. I received your letter from Yucatán.

Let me hear from you. Family spoke well of you.

                        As ever,
                        Bill

10.
March 12, 1954
Tanger

Dear Neal,

What has happened to Allen? I received one letter from Yucatán and have heard nothing since then. My letters to Mexico City were returned unclaimed.

If he is there tell him to write me at once. If not do you know where he is? Please let me hear from you right away as I am quite worried. Is Jack with you?

This town would please you. Weed absolutely legal, and you can smoke it anywhere.

Please write to me.

As ever,
Bill Burroughs
%U.S. Legation
Tanger
Morocco.

letters . . . returned unclaimed: A few letters concern A.G.'s several months' retirement near Miraflores Village in Peten Rainforest, a day's ride by boat and horseback from railroad town Salto de Agua, in Chiapas, Mexico. Mail communication was delayed a month at a time or more. See "Siesta in Xbalba" pp. 21–39, (*Reality Sandwiches*, City Lights, S.F., 1963) and pp. 49–53, *Journals Early 50's, Early 60's* (Grove Press, N.Y., 1977).

11.
April 7 [1954]
[Tanger]

Dear Allen,

I have written and rewritten this for you. So please answer.

Routines like habit. Without routines my life is chronic nightmare, gray horror of midwest suburb. (When I lived in St. Louis and drove home past the bare clay of subdivided lots, here and there houses set down on platforms of concrete in the mud, play-houses of children who look happy and healthy but empty horror and panic in clear gray-blue eyes, and when I drove by the subdivisions always felt impact in stomach of final loneliness and despair. This is part of Billy Bradshinkel story. I don't know whether it is parody or not.)

I have to have receiver for routine. If there is no one there to receive it, routine turns back on me and tears me apart, grows more and more insane (literal growth like cancer) and impossible, and fragmentary like berserk pinball machine and I am screaming: "Stop it! Stop it!"

Trying to write novel. Attempt to organize material is more painful than anything I ever experienced. Shooting every four hours. Some semi-synthetic stuff called Eukodol. God knows what kind of habit I am getting. When I kick this habit I expect fuses will blow out in my brain from overcharge and black sooty blood will run out eyes, ears and nose and staggering around the room acting out routines like Roman Emperor routine in a bloody sheet.

Notes on C: When you shoot C in main line—no other way of taking it gives the real C kick—there is a rush of pure pleasure to the head. Before you can clean the needle the pleasure dims. Ten minutes later you take another shot. No visceral pleasure, no increase of enjoyment, no sense of well-being, no alteration or widening or perspective. C is electricity through the brain stimulating pleasure connections that can only be known with C. (As now scientists put long needles into the brain—brain has no feeling—and directly stimulate centers of pleasure and pain with electric current. Idea for science fiction. Like a television set you attach electrodes to the brain and get broadcast of pure pleasure mixed with political indoctrination. Give that one to

Bradbury.) Once C channels are stimulated there is urgent desire to restimulate and fear of falling from C high. The urgency lasts as long as C channels are activated—an hour or so. Then you forget it because it corresponds to no pleasure ordinarily experienced. C is a specific substance not a means to any other enjoyment. There is no withdrawal syndrome with C. It is literally all in the mind, hideous need of the brain, a need without body and without feeling. Reversal of natural direction of current which is from the viscera that feel to the brain that does not.

In C high brain is berserk pinball machine flashing blue and pink connections in electric orgasm. Science fiction note—C pleasure could be felt by a mechanical brain. First stirrings of autonomous activity.

[Remainder of letter missing.]

12.
April 13 [1954]
[Tanger]

Dear Jack,

A P.S. to forward to Allen. Everything is going wrong here. My boy's family has beefed to the fuzz. Also have beef on junk. All in all it looks like I will be taking a little trip for a week or so. Continue to write me here however.

Weather is also bad here. Well let me hear from you. I can't seem to get anything done in the way of writing. Plans very uncertain. May go almost anywhere. I don't know at all what I am going to do. Everyone in Tanger bores me.

Love,
Bill

13.
May 2 [1954]
[Tanger]

Dear Neal,

I received letter from Allen dated April 9, and sent him some money in the form of traveller's checks. In his letter he said he was living on a finca (country estate) with a female archeologist. All in all I cannot think he is completely out of touch, and the return of your money may well have been simply a bureaucratic fuck up. If he were in jail he would certainly have communicated with the U.S. Consul in Mérida, and his death would certainly have been reported by now since he seemingly has friends: the archeologist who is American, and the owner of the hotel in Chiapas.

All in all I am inclined to think everything is quite O.K.

But there is some cause for worry to be sure. I think I had best write to his father, and ask him, if he has not had word recently, to check through U.S. Consul in Mérida, or through the Embassy in Mexico City. You always check through your consulate, never direct with Mexican officials

I will write to his father today. Meanwhile write me at once if anything develops. I will look into the books you mention.

                    As ever,
                    Love,
                    Bill

%U.S. Legation
  Tanger, Morocco

14.
May 2, 1954
Tanger

Dear Mr. [Louis] Ginsberg,

I am sorry to worry you, but have just received a rather alarming letter from Neal Cassady in California. It seems that Neal wired money to Allen on April 6th at Allen's urgent request. The money was returned unclaimed, and Neal has heard nothing since.

I received a letter from Allen dated April 9, in which he mentioned that he was waiting on money from Neal. I immediately wired my parents to send Allen $30 in convertible traveller's checks by air mail to the address he gave in Chiapas, the only address I have:

>Hotel Arturo Huy,
>Salto De Agua,
>Chiapas, Mexico.

In all probability Allen is all right. But if you have not heard from him recently, it might be indicated to write the U.S. Embassy in Mexico City—Protection Dept.—to check his whereabouts and welfare without delay. I think there is a consulate in Mérida, Yucatán, but the request should be addressed to The Embassy in Mexico City and they will take the necessary measures.

I know you do not fully approve of me, Mr. Ginsberg, but I hope you will believe that I have a deep and sincere friendship for Allen. If I was in the U.S. I would go to Mexico at once to find out what is wrong. I hope you will do me the favor of letting me know what you find out. I am very much worried and upset.

>Sincerely,
>William Burroughs

Address: Cargo U.S. Consulate
          Tanger, Morocco
          North Africa

P.S. I am, of course willing to do anything I can to help in this matter. If there is any question of a legal difficulty, the man to contact is Lic. Bernabe Jurado, 17 Madero St., Mexico City.

15.
May 2, 1954
[Tanger]

Dear Neal,

    I just wrote a letter to Allen's father suggesting he contact The Protection Dept., U.S. Embassy in Mexico City at once, they should check Allen's whereabouts. I addressed letter to: 416 East 34th Street, Paterson, N.J. You have heard from Allen's father recently. Is that the correct address? If not please address the enclosed letter to Allen's father and send along at once. I seem to remember Allen said something about his father having moved to another house. In any case I want to be sure he receives my letter and acts on it at once.

    You must understand that a request to the Embassy from a friend would in all probability be ignored. Any letters to police chiefs in Chiapas are worse than useless. Allen's father is the only one who can get action from the Embassy, and writing to him is only possible recourse.

                 Love,
                  Bill

% U.S. Legation
   Tanger.

16.
COBBLE STONE GARDENS

Laura Lee Burroughs   Mortimer Burroughs
   231 Phipps Plaza   Palm Beach, Florida

Monday May 17th 1954

Dear Allen,

We were greatly relieved to hear from you and to learn that you were all right except broke. Bill was so worried that he couldn't work so we sent him a cable this morning.

I am enclosing $50.00 in travellers checks payable to you. This is the way I always send money to Bill. He wanted me to do this for you.

. The money we wired to you at Salto de Agua was returned just after we had sent you the telegram.

               Sincerely,
               Mortimer Burroughs

17.
May 11 [1954]
[Tanger]

Dear Allen,

I arranged with an Englishman who is broke he should keep my clothes, bring me food, and dole out dollies for ten days. I am paying him fifty dollars. His name is Gifford. He seems to be a fairly right guy. I was shooting every two hours. There are no sanitariums here so this is the only way to arrange cure. This is second day and pretty rough. Yesterday I stole clothes from other boarder, sneaked out, and bought some Eukodol ampules and glutted myself. Gifford found out about it, confiscated the remaining ampules, and now the other boarder locks his door when he goes out, and Gifford also took my money. So I am really stuck now. I wish you were administering this cure. Gifford, he's a hard man. No use trying to coax an extra ampule out of him. "By God" he says "I'm being paid to do it and I'm going to do it right."

He just brought in a long letter from you from Chiapas. Sorry you didn't get the money I had sent. I did my best. I am afraid I made rather a fuss about your "disappearance," but Neal did write me he was sure you were either in jail or dead by a mule path.

I will send along two more letters. You haven't seen anything yet. There were even some letters I *destroyed* as too extreme.

I just thought of a scheme to lure an Arab into my room (easy enough, they are always knocking on the window). And get his clothes on pretext I have to go out and get money and all my clothes are in the laundry.

This would be a good place to build a house. You can get a lot for about $250. And building material is cheap.

Enclose beginning of novel. Glad to see we coincide on idea you should come here or anyhow we travel together somewhere. I am pretty fed up with travelling alone, and never meet any routine receivers and it is a bore without you. Well we will talk further on this matter.

Love,
Bill

P.S.   Note material in novel from letters.

18.
May 22 [1954]
[Tanger]

Dear Allen,

Just a quick note. Kells is here and sends his love. He is not looking at all well. Put on twenty pounds. Juices too much.

I hope none of my letters to you went astray. Some of them I addressed 1047 *Santa Clara*, neglecting to put in the *East* Santa Clara. So please let me know what letters you do have. I should have some code system so we could check. You should have by now about four or five long letters—eight to twelve pages—containing routines, part of a novel, soap operas, miscellanea. But four *considerable* communications which are part of work in progress. I have carbons of most of this material so will send copies if you are lacking anything. So please write me what you do have. If three letters are not waiting for you at Neal's you might check with post office.

My cure is over, but I am still taking about six dollies per day. I will have to be very firm with myself.

Let me know what the situation is in Frisco. I will stay here, where I can save money, until I know what you are planning to do.

Tanger would be ideal place to have a house and spend two or three months every year writing, plenty sex and costing about nothing to live. You can buy a small house in the native quarter for about $1500. Or build one outside town for about same amount.

I had wire from family you are all right. Allen, you can always contact them for aid in an emergency. I have told them that you are my best friend and they should help you the same as they would help me. Mother wrote me: "Why didn't Allen let us know he was in difficulties?"

Date with Kiki tonight. Junk-sick sexy. Wish you were here. Kells and I making trip to Kislit where are beautiful dancing girls. Sounds like ho-hum dept. so far as I am concerned.

Well, better mail this before I gather any momentum. Point of this letter is I want to be sure you have all the material I sent to you.

Love to Neal and congrats on $17,000.

Love,
Bill

P.S. Family wired you $30 to Salto which came back unclaimed. I sent $10 in a letter to Embassy in Mexico, D.F. Did you get the $10?

1047 E. Santa Clara: Neal Cassady's household address San Jose, California.

dollies: Refers to Dolophine (now commonly known as methadone) which Burroughs and other intelligent junkies used at the time to supplant heroin and other opiate habits, and for home reduction cure. It took U.S. Government a quarter-century to get around to same method and semi-legalize it.

Love to Neal and congrats on $17,000: Cassady had injured his ankle permanently, as railroad brakeman, in an athletic feat of breaking down or uncoupling a train speeding toward a wreck. In the lesser smashup his ankle was broken badly, and the sum mentioned as his injury compensation. An heroic deed.

19.
June 8   May 8 [1954]
really–AG/ more or less I
forget
[Tanger]

Dear Allen, (or should I dispense with these amenities and simply start the letter: Allen?) I was out of paper on the other letter. The typewriter is broke and Kells came and took it away. I think it was Kells. Somebody was in the room and the typewriter is gone.

The Río de Oro is inhabited by the Blue Men—so called because they are blue (blue *all over* he, he, typical queer *bon mot à la* Tanger. God what a lot of jerks live here.) They are blue because of a dye they use in their robes which gets in the skin and dyes the skin blue so that they are blue. Nobody has been back in the hinterland of Río de Oro. Two intrepid French explorers found "unspeakably mutilated," presumably by the Blue Men. A mysterious figure known as the Blue Sultan is key man in the area. Now I simply plan to go to the edge of Río de Oro, and see if I can get up any kind of an expedition to penetrate the hinterland, which is trackless desert with a few oasis cities. All in all I do not expect anything will come of it except a trip there and back. But you never know what may happen.

Well like I say I will wait until I kick habit before deciding anything.

Oh God I owe Jack $30 and don't have it to send him. He will be hounding me like Friendly Finance. I feel so guilty I can't bring myself to write to him.

I neglected to give Carl your address. Sorry, but we were walking to the terminal, and I was late. Marker is still looking for a job in Miami.

Love,
Bill

P.S. Did not see Holmes. Jack wants to show the Ms. to Cowley. I think this is last possibility so try everyone else first.

20.
June 24 [1954]
[Tanger]

Dear Allen,

I always like keep a letter to you on the stove and put in miscellaneous ideas, a sort of running diary. I've been thinking about routine as art form and what distinguishes it from other forms. One thing, it is not *completely symbolic*; that is, it is subject to shlup over into "real" action at any time. In a sense the whole Nazi movement was a great, humorless, evil *routine* on Hitler's part. Do you dig me? I am not sure I dig myself. And some pansy shit is going to start talking about *living* his art.

Last night went with Kells to extraordinary Arab restaurant that looked like remodeled bus station—bare, galvanized iron roof. A huge banana palm growing in this barn-like or hangar-like room with tables scattered here and there. Served by a snotty Arab queen who was barely courteous when we ordered two plates and one portion of Cous Cous. An Arab stew of chicken, nuts, raisons, and corn meal. Delicious. I was tea high and never got suck (leave error) taste kicks. We had just been in Dean's Bar, where I encountered barrage of hostility. Dean wanted not to serve me, rolling his eyes in disapproval, but there was Kells, a good customer. (Dean has heard that I am a dope fiend. More than that he instinctively feels me as danger, far out, an ill omen.) So I sat there, loaded on tea, savoring their disapproval, rolling it on my tongue with glass of good dry sherry.

Really cutting down on junk and sooo sexy. Kiki coming tonight.

Got letter from my Portuguese mooch. They are locking his grandmother out of her iron lung for non-payment of rent. The finance co. is repossessing his wife's artificial kidney. Up his with a grapefruit. I am really toughening up on mooches. Bastards who wouldn't give *anything*—to me most of all not. That's mooch psychology: they most especially wouldn't help people who helped them. Well

I've subsidized my last mooch. From here on out all my money I need for myself, my few friends, and the few people like Kiki and Angelo who have been right with me.

Most secure form of security is friends who would help you *unconditionally.* You know so long as I have anything, you have part of it. So long as I have a place to stay, so do you. That is really something can't be bought, Allen.

Let's get on with this novel. Maybe the real novel is letters to you.

Love,
Bill

21.
June 25 [1954]
Tanger

Dear Allen,

Your daily page. I hope all the essential briefs on my case were waiting for you in Frisco, so we won't have that hang-up of letters crossing and counter-crossing, but more or less definite statements taking into consideration all the angles.

I am writing some really wild pornography for relaxation. Will send along when is in good shape. Most pornography has no interest because the personnel involved are mechanized, inhuman, drearily dull like the dramatis personae in dirty movies and photos. Did I ever tell you about the time I went to dirty movies in Mexico City whorehouse and I had lost my glasses and I said: "If that isn't the hairiest son of a bitch I ever see fucking that cunt." Wind-up is it's a *dog*, a German police dog.

This is Kiki's Saint day when all his friends give him

presents. I told him: "Kiki I'm going to do something *real* nice for you."

"Yes? . . . What?" Expecting a wrist watch at least.

"I'm going to give you the best screwing you ever had!"

That's a routine I have from Texas, quoted from old, rich oil man to young wife.

I did, of course, give him presents. Nylon socks, underwear, a knife, a tooth brush. I am surrounded by curious Kafkian hostility. A number of people seem to have taken a violent, irrational dislike to me. Especially people who run bars. I am a bad sign and no mistake. When you see Willy Lee sitting at the bar, your trap has had it. This is *not* imagination, Allen.

Tanger is a marrowbone conventional town. Any one far-out threatens this moneychanging town. It is also a *psychic* money-changing town. People go *conventional* mad here, like Malcolm the Name Dripper (he *drips* names like a gonorrhea cock drips pus) is now beside himself because he wheedled introduction to Cary Grant out of Tennessee Williams. Williams probably says: "Well see if you can shake him. I couldn't." You dig Malcolm is out and out *mad*. He thinks these people like and accept him. What a *dreary* madness! Jane Bowles asks people: "Who *are* you?"

The place is Kwakiutl, potlack, competitive humiliating mad. Any one comes on straight, sincere, unarmoured is hated. Like looking right into someone's eyes, feeling momentary warmth for him (perhaps a little drunk or tea high or junked up), I have frequently encountered sheer black hate. It scares me. Not the hate itself but the condition that underlies it. (Again I feel myself falling short of what I want to say.) No snotty uptown fags can compare with these for utter, pretentious, insincere, inhuman snobishness. To give you a sample, Kells goes to *The Parade* where the elegant fags hang. He starts conversation with man next to him at the bar. The man answers in short sentences then lets conversation lapse.

Kells: You come here direct from the States?
Fag: No, from Brazil.
Kells: So? And how did you come?
Fag: By yacht, *of course.*

That really takes the rag off the bush. Surrounded by these monsters, I feel understandably alone and frightened and need the help of my few friends more than usual.

How did your camera work out? Do you get good pictures with it? Send me sample if you have one appropriate. Did you get the photos I sent? Did you get the dream routine (not a routine exactly) about rusty iron City of the future? Did you get the ten dollars? Did you leave forwarding address at Embassy in Mex. D. F. so they will send mail right along? I often spent like a week working 10 to 15 hours a day on one of those ten-page letters to you. So, I want to be sure you get them all, and if not will send copies. Especially I want to be *sure* you have the City Dream. It's four pages.

Love,
Bill

22.
July 3 [1954]
[Tanger]

Dear Allen,

I am really ill. Pain and swelling in the joints. I ask the captain what it could be . . . "Oh" he says "I *hope* it isn't a bone fell."

"A what?"

"An infection of the bone. See that scar? I had the same thing once and they had to cut down and scrape off the bone . . . Of course maybe it isn't that at all . . . maybe it's just nothing and then *on the other hand* it may be arthritis or God knows what awful thing!"

"I never had arthritis or anything like that."

"Well there's always a first time . . . Oh it's probably nothing. But then you never can tell . . ."

So here I am sick and broke and Kells left for Madrid this morning. Hope to God I don't get laid up here. I want to get out of Tanger . . . Would like to go straight to Denmark . . . Unless I can get a job in Madrid . . . But this place drags me like a sea anchor . . . Just took a short walk to see if I could find someone to talk to and give me a lift. Two people looked the other way quickly. I don't like either one of them in any case . . . Then I met Eric who is one of those people pursued by almost incredible bad luck. I don't feel up to recounting the saga of Eric The Unlucky, beyond to say that he is 50, no job, no money, no prospects, an eighty-year-old mother to support . . . Tanger is full of people like that, sort of washed up here. The sight of him brought me down the rest of the way. No use telling myself this is not nothing. Pain worse by the minute . . . Eric has a hard luck story worth three of that, like the time he got septicemia from an abdominal abcess and they put him in a Syrian hospital, and the Greek surgeon goofed and sewed up a live monkey inside him—and he was gang fucked by the Arab attendants . . . Or the self-righteous English Doctor who gave him an enema of hot sulphuric acid for the clap . . . Or the German Practitioner who removed his appendix with an old, rusty can opener and tin shears: "The germ theory is a nonsense." Flushed with success, he then began snipping and cutting out everything in sight: "The human body is most inefficient machine. Filled up vit unnecessitated parts . . . You can get by with von kidney—vy have two? Yes dot is a kidney. The inside parts should not be so close in together crowded. They need Lebensraum, like der Vaterland . . ." This German cat practices something he calls technological medicine. This has got worse while I wrote the letter. Now I can hardly move . . . Kiki is here . . . If I am not better tomorrow, will see if I can score for a good croaker . . . Tanger is known for its bad doctors . . . Kiki comes on more affectionate all the time . . . a real sweet kid. He is helping me get my clothes off.

I can just barely make it around the room, my ankle hurts so . . . I must see a doctor tomorrow . . . what a bum kick to die in this awful place!

—Will write in morning again how I feel . . .

Morning—still can't walk or just barely . . . will try and get a croaker here. Send this letter via the captain.

Love,
Bill

P.S. What gives with Neal's spiritualism? You never mentioned it.

[The captain: an ex-captain drummed out of the service because of his homosexual tendencies.]

The German Practitioner: A precursor of Dr. Benway.

Neal's Spiritualism: A study of Edgar Cayce's ideas on reincarnation that became obsessional, driving Kerouac to Dwight Goddard's *Buddhist Bible* to study the oriental origins of Western pop-spiritual notions.

23.
July 8 Thursday [1954]
[Tanger]

Dear Allen,

I have been very ill for the past week. Joints painful and swollen. Light fever. Deep lassitude.

My check unaccountably delayed and I haven't a cent.

I don't feel up to hassle of trying to promote medicine and doctor on credit. Living past five days on bread and tea, and not much bread.

Have cut junk almost to vanishing point and don't miss it, I am that sick. (Wrote long letter to you but when I read it over it bored me so I won't send it. Don't know when I will have money to send this letter.)

Kells is in Madrid presumably looking over job situation.

Kiki has been with me throughout my illness, fixing me soup and tea, sitting with me and stroking my head, and tucking me in. (Remember I am broke now and have no money to give him.) Find me an American kid like that. Not that they are easy to come by any place, but Angelo in Mexico was very similar. What I feel with them is not the same as what I feel with you, but it is definitely a *relationship*. That is, involves real affection on both sides and some protoplasmic contact. In U.S. such relations are always straining to be something more or different from what they in fact are, with resulting unease for both parties. Actually U.S. provides no counterpart to my relation with Kiki or Angelo . . .

I sleep twenty hours a day. Continual nightmares. Like wake up perhaps in nuthouse ward twenty years from now. Flabby and toothless and old, or *horribly changed* in some way, some place. Nightmares of *feeling* without clear content. Feel great formless menace pressing on me. Kiki says I talk all the time in my sleep. He sits here reading most of the day. I always wake up with start of fear. Sometimes with a cry.

The European trip was ill-omened. I knew it as soon as I dug that awful Greek boat, then Italy with the baths closed, prices high, cold so I never got warm in Rome. The strange hostility I have encountered here. People I don't even know profess violent dislike for me—I want to terminate the trip as soon as possible. But I will try to take in Denmark.

Kiki has gone off duty for the night and I feel lonely and frightened. Even if I felt fine and had money there is nobody here for me to talk to, nothing to do, no place to go. This place is like a wind-swept Tierra del Fuego. Literally and figuratively. The water is shock cold in mid-summer (some fucking cold current.) The beach is unusable because of the winds that create a continual sandstorm there, so that the hardy fruits who *do* sit all day on the beach are always digging sand out of their red eyes.

The real disappointment of European trip is: I have met no one who is anywhere. More than that, I feel myself out of place, unwanted; missing what, if anything, *is* here.

Just reading over with great interest your dream of the Dark Knight from Chiapas letter. Could you clarify? That letter is confusing. I can't tell what is dream. I can't tell where dream leaves off and fact or comment takes over. I enclose some tea high material has been kicking around some time.

Friday July 9

No check this morning. If nothing in afternoon mail I am stuck over weekend with no doctor, no food, and no junk. I have cut way down on junk, but don't know how sick I may be when I stop altogether. I dread a withdrawal depression at this point. No check, but put it to the captain for 50 pesetas ($1.25). That will have to last me the next two days.

Sat. Morning July 10

Kiki and Angelo both have mark of bad luck and failure. Both honest, loyal, willing to work, but no specialized abilities. They are *too nice* to be successful. They are incapable of faking or insincerity. I used to feel in Angelo, and now in Kiki, some of the same deep discouragement and hopelessness with the System I feel in myself.

Just came across this in my papers. I had forgotten I

wrote it. It looks good so I pass along: "Never worry or think like 'I have to organize this novel, save money, go here or there.' These things will arrange themselves if you do not interfere and let your deepest desires shape circumstances. All you can do is see that your deep needs are freed from constraint. Once that is done, you have no need to worry and you have nothing to say about what happens. Like meeting people. You will meet someone or not. That is fatalism connected with the *facts* of space/time positions and tracks. Literally: you are there or you are not there.

"The Huabdropoza Indians of Orinoco, who live in darkest jungle and flee from light. On lowest plane of existence, but show signs of intelligence. 'Strange, pathetic desires and emotions pass over their faces' (Quote from French explorer) What a kick to adopt one and mold him to specifications, or what would happen?

"It is essential to do these things now while there is time. I mean studies of the hostile and queer indians and of those who are excessively timid and fear the light. Also I must write this queer novel. I am only one who can write it. I have a duty to do these things."

Would God I had something to *eat*. I mean I am so tired of bread and tea. The sight of it nauseates me. Now it is time for my supper: a slice of bread without butter, and tea with no sugar.

Sunday, July 11

Worse this morning. I can hardly walk and much pain in right ankle which is swollen out sleek and red, you can't feel the bone. I love to run my hand over it. It's so smooth and taut. *I must see a doctor tomorrow* under any circumstances. Wake up junk-sick and in pain. I had to borrow fifty cents and buy some ampules of dolophine (last shot 16 hours before). But I really have cut down to very little. If there is no check tomorrow that means definitely the letter is lost. I will have to sell my suitcase and whatever else I can scrape together, and send a telegram to family they should wire me money. The last thing I would sell is this typewriter.

Now even Kiki has deserted me. He hasn't been here all day, just when I have a relapse and can't walk and need help. I wanted to arrange with him to sell my effects for me tomorrow if I don't get my check . . . I am feverish and chilled. Going back to bed.

Love,
Bill

P.S. Money came today (Monday). Saw a good German croaker. Rheumatic fever. Just like me to contract an adolescent illness. *Heart not yet affected.* Another few days might have been different story. I could never have promoted the medicine on credit in this cheap, miserable town. Doc says I will be walking in two days with some new anti-rheumatic shit they got. Right now I can't walk two steps. Kiki back on the job.

Best to Neal,
Love,
Bill

I must have lost 15 pounds in the past week with fever and no food. Weight down to 125 pounds, more or less. Remember fever I had in N.Y.? It was a touch of the same thing.

What about Neal's spiritualism kick? I want to hear the details.

Dream of Dark Night from Chiapas letter: A.G. had dreamt of a knight at end of journey. "No tragedy like that of the dark hero who comes to the end of his journey to kneel before an image he discovers to be *not* of his own heart's desire."

24.
Letter completed   *July 15 [1954]*
Wednesday July 22   *Thursday*
                                         [Tanger]

Dear Allen,

Still confined to my room and sleep most of the time. I am completely unproductive. Haven't written a word. Feel deep heaviness and lassitude, like I have been five minutes writing these few lines. In fact decided to go back to sleep and finish letter later.

The doctor was just here. Heart O.K. Secondary infection in the right ankle which will have to be punctured and drained. How tiresome. Now I have to prepare a hot poultice for my ankle, and the thought of it exhausts me. I will wait until tomorrow when Kiki comes and he will do it.

Friday Morning July 16

The doctor came today and tapped my ankle, drawing out a jigger glass full of pus. This is a secondary infection which will necessitate a course of penicillin. The rheumatism is seemingly cured. I can consider myself very lucky in that I left an acute attack of rheumatic fever for a week without treatment and suffered no damage to the heart. Many people are invalided for life by such an attack, which leads me to observe that I do generally have good luck in matters of basic importance.

Just sent Kiki to the Embassy, and he brought back a long letter from you which has roused me from this lethargy. I think your suggestion of writing after receiving a letter is a good one and will tend to avoid confusion and to come closer to the ideal of letter writing, which is to communicate with someone who is not there. I will follow this practice in the future.

And Hoeniger: I explained to him ten times at least that *all* Colombian tourist cards are signed by the Consul, and subsequently relegated by him to airlines and travel agencies for distribution to travellers. So that in a sense, all tourist cards are issued by the Consul. But I never saw the Consul, the card was given me by the man who sold me my airline ticket, who was, *ipso facto*, an authorized representative of the airline. What could be simpler? But he says he can do nothing because the card was issued by the Consul. And Phyllis Jackson losing Jack's manuscript. What is wrong with these people? If I ever launch a commercial enterprise I shall stipulate only those without business experience need apply for work. I would not care to struggle wth a staff of idiots.

Tibetan Buddhism is extremely interesting. Dig it if you have not done so. I had some mystic experiences and convictions when I was practicing Yoga. That was 15 years ago. Before I knew you. My final decision was that Yoga is no solution for a Westerner and I disapprove of all practice of Neo-Buddhism. Yoga should be practiced, yes, but not as final, a solution, but rather as we study history and comparative cultures. The metaphysics of Jiu-jitsu is interesting, and derives from Zen. If there is Jiu-jitsu club in Frisco, join. It is worthwhile and one of the best forms of exercise, because it is predicated on relaxation rather than straining. I am anxious to read all the material on Cayce, and will do so. But that must wait.

My ankle is still swollen. The doctor says some restriction of movement may persist, may in fact be permanent. The thing was unfortunately neglected. However the fever and infection are seemingly cured. Thanks for your offer of medicines. Tanger seems pretty well supplied with the latest products. Unlike Greece where, according to Kells, there is difficulty procuring the most common drugs. It occurs to me diagnosing could be done very well by a thinking machine. You feed in the symptoms and out come all possible conditions that could produce that syndrome. For example Doctor Perone never thought of rheumatic fever because the rheumatic symptoms were hardly perceptible. Thinking back now, I recall joint pain at that time.

I have written to Kerouac asking for those addresses in Paris. If I get them I will likely go from here to Paris—boat to Marseille skipping Spain—in next two weeks. For intellectual stimulation Tanger is nowhere. There are a few writers here, mostly friends of Bowles, who seemingly wants nothing to do with me. It has occurred to me that Bowles perhaps wishes to avoid contact with me because of my narcotic associations, fearing possible hassles with customs inspection and authorities in general if he is known to be on familiar terms with me—guilt by association. I don't know.

[Remainder of letter missing.]
Phyllis Jackson losing Jack's Ms.: An agent to whom *On the Road* was entrusted lost it for some months in an office closet in the giant MCA Agency.

25.
August 18 [1954]
Tanger

Dear Allen,

I enclose carbon copy of letter to Jack which covers partially recent developments. Still trying to book passage without success. Really I don't know what to do. Burfurd did not answer my note. I have no assurance of finding anybody in Paris. Trip would likely be expensive fiasco. On other hand tired of Tanger, have no friends here—no prospect of making any. In regard to your suggestion about contacting Bowles: recall that I have already met him, that he knows very well who I am (I have this from the captain who has tea with Bowles from time to time). So by all indications he does not want to see me for reasons of his own.

I am not a Reichian, but I feel very strongly that the

Christian concept of Sin is a blight on the earth that has occasioned incalculable misery. I am sorry to see Neal oriented in that dreary direction.

I am having trouble with my writing. I can well understand your difficulties in seeking a suitable *form* for your poems. I have the same trouble, which led me to experiment with a new language. No I never got beyond *atua*. Too much trouble.

I am so eager to see you. Hope to God I can score for a berth before October! By the way I rather fancy my description of sex with Kiki in letter to Jack. Also my dissertation on Buddhism. Jack tells me Frisco has extremely active vice squad, with cops arresting junkies on every corner. What is U.S. coming to? For a long-range plan I want to build or buy a house somewhere outside the States and live there at least half of every year. A place where I can live cheap and write, and my friends can visit indefinitely. *Where*? I can't decide. Tanger has all the sex you want, it is cheap, and you are not a foreigner here. That is, you have the same rights as anybody, can go into business if you want to. In trouble with the law the cops usually side with an American. In fact they have orders not to bother us except, of course, if caught in commission of some major crime. I mean we are exempt from questioning, arrest on suspicion, any legal interference with our private lives. The cop here is what he *should be every place*: an agent to maintain order and protect property. M. Watson's drive against "homosexualism" was stillborn.

I suppose you have been reading about the "unrest" in Morocco. So far no trouble here but it is expected momentarily. Tomorrow is the bad day, anniversary of day the old Sultan was spirited away by the French (a ridiculous expression, "spirited away," come to think). And me caught short without a pistol the one time in my life I really need one! If I only had my *curare* at least I could buy game darts and smear them with *curare*. As it is, I bought a meat cleaver and a razor-sharp knife. I live right in the Native Quarter, but around the corner from a police station. Last riot in Tanger was in '52; twelve Arabs were killed by the police, and an unfortunate Swiss tourist was torn in pieces by the Arab mob under the misapprehension he was French. Tomorrow after the noon prayer hour is when trouble is expected. We will see.

You recall my short story about the car accident with Jack A.? I have rewritten it completely and will send along a copy either enclosed or under separate cover.

Did you receive the three photos I sent you from the new camera? If so, tell me what you think of them.

I killed a large rat tonight in the kitchen, with the cane I used when cripped by rheumatism. Tony went in hysterics. I felt so *manly*.

As regards that story you might try placing it, I don't know just where. The profane portion can be excised with no great loss. However I can't think of any magazine that would be interested, though it is, unlike most of my writing, in conventional short story form.

Incidentally I also have a weapon of my own devising I think is rather clever. It is a round piece of lead about two inches in diameter attached by a socket to a short piece of cord I loop around my wrist. I can throw it at short range and then recover it to use again, or simply swing it on a short length of the cord. The advantage is it can be used at a distance beyond the reach of a weapon in a man's hand, and then used again. Another of my inventions is a flit gun full of ammonia. All these weapons are in case a mob tries to force their way into the house (but I carry the knife now in the street). Well if Mr. Watson is attending to his business nothing will happen. They have a hundred troops in readiness, and the police are armed with submachine guns. They would likely be as much a menace to us as to the Arabs, when they start spraying bullets around these narrow streets that all lead around in a circle. You could fire a bullet in one side of the Kasbah and it would ricochet around corners and come out the other end.

Kiki and I spent one of our delightful afternoons today, lying on the bed naked, dozing and making desultory love, smoking a little *kif*, and eating great, sweet grapes. What a tranquil, healthy young male he is! There doesn't seem to be a conflict in him. Angelo was the same way, but I didn't appreciate him as I would now. Contrast Kiki with someone like Jack A., with all those grating conflicts and feelings of inferiority so well grounded in fact and so utterly hopeless, depressing one with the whole unsavory mess. Kiki would be quite at home in "sophisticated" company. He simply wouldn't try to compete. The only danger would be that he would be pampered and spoiled. Example of his health and simplicity: he had some sort of infection or swelling in his rectum, and I gave him four shots of penicillin. The other day he was sitting on the bed naked and I asked him if his ass was all right. "Yes" he said with a boyish grin, and putting his hands on his knees rolled himself back showing me his ass. It was done without a trace of prissiness *or* exhibitionism, beyond a natural joy in his body that any young human male has. As you say, he is a dream for which I will have nostalgia. Hard to duplicate in the States.

Let me repeat that I am *not* basically paranoid, that is I do not have the character structure of true paranoia. I am fundamentally quite reasonable and have sense of fact unusually well developed. Nonetheless my state of soul is very bad indeed. I don't altogether know what is wrong. I know that I am subject to horrible despair, so if I had the money would go immediately to nearest sanitarium (Casablanca). Afraid just can't make it outside. Kiki has given up. One thing is sure though. I will be habitless by the time I reach Frisco. So don't worry about that.

Got off the track of where I want my house if and when. Like I say Tanger is subject to change, the Arabs might get all Morocco, or the fucking Spanish might grab Tanger. They always wanted it. Kiki's father was killed by the Fascists in the civil war. When they occupied Tanger they shot all the Republican supporters they could find.

And America supports that lousy bastard who is no better than Hitler! What a complete non-entity Eisenhower turned out to be! Do you know in the past two years 2000 people have been dismissed from the State Department Foreign Service—only twelve for Communism? The rest for being queer. What is the U.S. coming to? A police state. It really looks bad. So Tanger is unstable, and I don't like the foreign colony, and there isn't much to do (lousy beach, no hunting, no place to go.). Mexico is possibility, but you would have to have property in a Mexican's name. Even so you are always subject to be deported. I have thought of the West Indies, an area I don't know well, or even a compromise on Key West. We might make this a communal enterprise, you and Jack helping me to build the house. I am quite confident I can build one. Nothing to it. I mean we would like own the house in common and spend as much time there as we felt like, writing and living cheap. Somewhere on ocean is indicated in many ways—swimming, health, cheap fish, or catch your own. Something to think about.

    I may (one chance in a hundred) get on a Yugoslav freighter day after tomorrow. I won't know until the boat gets here whether it is full, and then it sometimes leaves in three hours, sometimes a week or more. I have made amazing discovery. When I am high with Miss Green, and lying next to Kiki, I get ideas faster and better than at other times. It's like he is some kind of orgone battery that tunes me in. I have tested this many times. The difference is palpable. Trouble is I don't feel like, and it isn't appropriate, to get up and write them down. Though I have written some down and they are always good. I mean he is sort of a *medium* through which I get ideas, especially when I am with Miss Green (though this is not essential) and preferably lying down together, not talking. We siesta together most every afternoon. He says he can't sleep at home because his brother bothers him and his mother keeps yelling at him: "Get outa here and get me some money too." She is quite reconciled to our relationship, since Kiki kicks in for household expenses. He says he sleeps special good with me, and we sleep about four hours every afternoon, all wrapped around each other as described in the letter to Jack. Sometimes we have sex, sometimes not. I find affectionate contact almost as satisfactory without sex. I believe Doctor Sullivan of the Washington School postulates an "intimacy need". I certainly feel a definite need for non-sexual intimacy, I don't mean *necessarily* non-sexual, you understand. I notice that Kiki seems to regard that as quite natural, whereas Americans have this let's-do-it-and-get-it-over-with attitude. In fact Kiki feels more affectionate than sexual towards me, so far as I can judge. Before his mother cracked down we used sometimes to spend sixteen hours in bed in close contact. Well I will try to get the story in this letter or at least in the same mail. It is quite different and I think much better. In present form I like it.

                Love,
                 Bill

P.S. Come to think of it the Tanger police are a model for just what police should be and do. They don't care at all about your sex life or whether you take junk (of course everybody smokes tea in the street like tobacco.). All they do is maintain order (and do a pretty thorough job too.) I haven't seen many fights and when a fight occurs the police are there in a matter of seconds. They were however not able to prevent a murder that occurred recently in the main drag, but there was no warning. One Arab walked up to another and stuck a knife in his stomach. And prevent theft (there is not much of that either).

    In an altercation an American is automatically right against an Arab. I like that, and I don't abuse it. If I hit someone you can be sure he deserves to be hit, because I am normally good-natured and easy-going to a fault. It is nice to know the cops will take your side if you do have trouble. I haven't had any to speak of here. One Arab tried to rob me, but a good hard shove ended the attempt. The tribunals don't even make a pretence of not discriminating. An Arab always draws more time than a European for the same offence. All sentences here are relatively light, however—5 years about maximum.

[Remainder of letter missing.]

26.
Aug. 18 [1954]
[Tanger]

Dear Jack,

Thanks for your letter providing me with Paris addresses. I wrote a note to Bob Burford identifying myself, and asking would he be in Paris, since I wanted to see him. No answer. Perhaps he is no longer at that address. I have generally received a cool reception in Europe and Tanger. The one time I met Paul Bowles he evinced no cordiality. Since then he has made no efforts to follow up the acquaintance. Perhaps he has some idea that trouble might result from anyone associated with narcotics. Since Tennessee Williams and Capote etc. are friends of Bowles, I, of course, don't meet them when they come here.

So far as I am concerned, ready to go home—but every line I have contacted so far is booked solid until October. Have various travel agencies working on the deal, but it doesn't look good. I wanted to travel with you to Frisco, joining Allen and Neal to work on R. Roads or something to save money so I can make expedition to S.A. jungles. Well I will make it as soon as I can.

Kiki has confiscated all my clothes and intends to cure me of the habit. I also have various new substitute preparations prescribed to me by a good German Jewish refugee doctor. So I have hopes of success with Kiki here to care for me, and to provide the appropriate amenities when I start coming off in my pants (I have no pants)—spontaneous orgasms being one of the few agreeable features of the withdrawal syndrome. And you are not limited to one orgasm. You can continue, with adolescent ardor, through three or four climaxes. Usually you are too weak to go out and find a "love object"—when you are coming off the junk, I mean, you don't feel up to looking around for sex—as the analysts call them. Sounds so passionless, like "I found a pretty hot object last night". I find myself getting jealous of Kiki—he is beseiged by importuning queens. In fact I am downright involved, up to my neck in Maya. He is a sweet kid, and it is so pleasant to loll about in the afternoon smoking tea, sleeping and having sex with no hurry, running leisurely hands over his lean, hard body and finally we doze off, all wrapped around each other, into the delicious sleep of a hot afternoon in a cool, darkened room, a sleep that is different from any other sleep, a twilight in which I savour, with a voluptuous floating sensation, the state of sleep, feeling the nearness of Kiki's young body, the sweet, imperceptible drawing together in sleep, leg inching over leg, arm encompassing body, hips hitching closer, stiffening organs reaching out to touch warm flesh. Jack, I would think twice before giving up sex. It's a basic kick and when it's good as it can be, it's *good*.—Sounds like literary marriage of Gertrude Stein and Hemingway.

I can't help but feeling that you are going too far with your absolute chastity. Besides, masturbation is *not* chastity, it is just a way of sidestepping the issue without even approaching the solution. Remember, Jack, I studied and practiced Buddhism (in my usual sloppy way to be sure). The conclusion I arrived at—and I make no claims to speak from a state of enlightenment, but merely to have attempted the journey, as always with inadequate equipment and knowledge (like one of my South American expeditions), falling into every possible accident and error, losing my gear and my way, shivering in cosmic winds on a bare mountain slope above life-line, chilled to the blood-making marrow with final despair of aloneness: What am I doing here, a broken eccentric, a Bowery Evangelist, reading books on Theosophy in the public library—(an old tin trunk full of notes in my cold water East Side flat)—imagining myself a Secret World Controller in Telepathic Contact with Tibetan Adepts . . . Could I ever see the merciless, cold facts on some Winter night, sitting in the operation room white glare of a cafeteria—NO SMOKING PLEASE—See the facts and myself, an old man with the wasted years behind, and what ahead having seen The Facts? A trunk full of notes to dump in a Henry St. lot? . . . So my conclusion was that Buddhism is only for the West to study as *history*, that is it is a subject for *understanding*, and Yoga can profitably be practiced to that end. But it is not, for the West, *an Answer*, not *a Solution*. We must learn by acting, experiencing, and living; that is, above all, by *Love* and by *Suffering*. A man who uses Buddhism or any other instrument to remove love from his being in order to avoid suffering has committed, in my mind, a sacrilege comparable to castration. You were given the power to love in order to use it, not matter what pain it may cause you. Buddhism frequently amounts to a form of psychic junk . . . I may add that I have seen nothing from those California Vedantists but a lot of horse shit, and I denounce them without cavil, as a pack of pathetic frauds. Convinced of their own line to be sure, thereby adding self–deception to their other failings. In short, a sorry bunch of psychic retreaters from the dubious human journey. Because if there is one thing I feel sure of it is this: that human life has *direction*—Even if we accept some Spenglerian Cycle routine, the cycle never comes back to exactly the same place, nor does it ever exactly repeat itself. Well, about enough of that. I am about to become a long-winded German with some philosophy about the direction of life arising from the potentials inherent in the cellular structure of the human time–space traveller. When the potentials of any species are exhausted, the species becomes static (like all animals, reptiles and other so-called lower forms of life). What distinguished Man from all other species is that he *cannot become static.* "*Er muss streben oder untergehen.*" (quote is from me)—"He must continue to develop or perish." This is going to run to five tremendous volumes. What I mean is the California Buddhists are trying to sit on the sidelines and there are no sidelines. Whether you like it or not, you are committed to the human endeavor. I cannot ally myself with such a purely negative goal as avoidance of suffering. Suffering is a chance you have to take by the fact of being alive. I repeat, *Buddhism is not for the West.* We must evolve our own solutions. If you don't enjoy sex, try an analyst. Some of them are good. I'd like to have a go with a Reichian myself. You might find yourself caught up in some tremendous D.H. Lawrence affair with a woman, orgasms together and all that. Well enough of abstract subjects. I am having serious difficulties with my novel. I tell you the novel form is completely inadequate to express what I have to say. I don't know if I can find a form. I am very gloomy as to prospects of publication. And I'm not like you, Jack, I need an audience. Of course, a small audience. But still I need publication for development. A writer can be ruined by too much or too little success. Looking at your letter again, I am dubious of finding any of these people since Burford does not reply (he may yet). Like I say, whole European trip has been unsuccessful. I have met no one anywhere. I feel myself out of place and unwanted wherever I go. So I am dubious of Paris. It is very expensive. If I didn't make contact with anybody, and this trip has been filled with such fantastic twists of ill luck, from the moment I stepped on that awful, dirty Greek boat. The signs just ain't right.

Like here I have nobody to talk to except Kiki. Some artist and writer colony! Oh yes there are two people who think I am a character I should be in television. Kiki is slowly denuding me of my clothes. He enjoys them so much and I care so little.

[Remainder of letter missing.]

Bob Burford: A founder of *Paris Review*, old acquaintance of Jack's from Denver 1947.

27.
August 26 [1954]
[Tanger]

Dear Allen,

I have made definite reservation to leave on the Italian line Sept. 7 from Gibraltar. Paris is out. No $ to go there, no reply from Burford. No way out by North route until mid-October.

The following is transcript from earlier letter which will show a definite progression and change of attitude:

Most definitive reason to stay here is Kiki. Lately I want him with me all the time. I found out last night that I love him. He comes in late last night. I had been sleeping, still drowsy, not digging exactly what he says. Suddenly I realize he is describing in ghastly detail the designs he proposes to have tattooed on the beautiful copper-brown skin of his chest and shoulders and arms. I run my hands over it by the hour while he purrs in sleep like a contented cat.

So had hysterics, cried, and kissed and begged him not to do it. "It's like you were going to put a plug in your lip, or a ring in your nose, or knocked out your front teeth to put in gold teeth—" (some of the Arabs do this)—It's a desecration!" He was finally impressed by my intensity. I gave him my last sport coat and my other pair of pants—(I have nothing left now but my combat jacket, one pair of slacks, and that odd sort of costume jewelry cheap brown coat from the chic-est shop on Worth Ave., in Palm Beach)—and $10 I could ill afford, to *promise* me *never* to have himself tattooed. I was shocked into an awareness that in a way I love him. Now I know I should not allow myself to be emotionally involved. He doesn't understand and looks at me in bewilderment when I embraced him with special intensity.

It is exasperating. I can't really get near him. I feel all-out attempt to do so would be disastrous for me. I know I should let matters rest in status of liaison, fond of him in an off-hand way, but it's so dull like that. I notice that sex is much more enjoyable since I feel some variety of love for him.

I am deeply distressed to hear of your difficulties, especially since they sound like the sort of thing nothing can be done about, a *cul-de-sac* of the soul. Couldn't you be happy, for example, with someone like Kiki? (His brows are not *bushy*, just copious, but in a pefectly symmetrical, straight-line arrangement. It's an Indian characteristic, and don't know where from, but Kiki looks like a South American Indian.) Sweet and affectionate, but indubitably masculine? Of course he is never going to fall madly in love with *you*. That's obvious. Incidentally Kiki isn't always sweet by any means. He can be sulky, and sometimes he shocks me with tirades of abuse. At such times find myself faced by a hostile stranger. Once he reduced me to tears. —I have always a fear with anyone I love that they really hate me and I will suddenly be confronted with their hate. Kiki always says afterward he was only joking.

I rewrote the story about the car wreck with Jack A. I think it is quite good in present form, one of the most nearly perfect things I have done. I think it may be publishable, and send along two versions—one cut for magazine consumption, the other containing a profane anecdote perhaps as well omitted. The symbol of the car interior, conveying illusion of security while hurtling towards inevitable disaster, is central. I have four alternative phrasings which I submit for your judgement. I have worked over it so much I can't judge. I choose number four for magazine version. Please try and sell this story some place as I think it is saleable.

       Love,
       Bill

P.S. One learns nothing by experience but caution, if you *want* to learn that. I don't, because that way you defeat yourself, removing the pleasure with the pain so the whole manoeuvre is pointless. I was just trying to sell you a deal like Kiki . . . Now I don't know. I am sick of being wise and Mahatmaish about love, when it just looks to me like a ghastly mess with only one consistent pattern, hurt and frustration. All this talk about how it is never wasted and you will get it all back one day, a good fairy is stashing it away some place and it is drawing interest and will all roll in with your Social Security payments. I am just writing along to put off the misery I will feel when I stop writing.

      28.
     August 30 [1954]
      [Tanger]

Dear Allen,
 At this point you should write no more to Tanger, as I leave here Sept. 7. Please write to me Cargo Jack.

In the past week the House of Tony has been visited by a plague of black rats. I dispatched two with my cane, and the Captain's Orderly—an insolent, ill-favored, little Arab pup—killed a third in the toilet, having armed himself with a Coca Cola bottle. A disquieting theory to explain presence of a rat in the toilet was advanced by Eric the Unlucky: they crawl and swim through the drains, emerging from the toilet bowl. Not a thought conducive to tranquil shitting.

Whatever is the matter with me? I can't seem to write anything. Not a word since *Driving Lesson*. Novel bogged down. My room and papers are in a mess that seems hopeless. I try to sort and classify, but the wind-up is moving papers from one place to another, like old, mad Mr. Elvins used to wake up in the middle of the night and move all his books from one end of the room to other.

[Remainder of letter missing.]

29.
Sept. 3 [1954]
[Tanger]

Dear Allen,

Do you have my story *Driving Lesson* I sent to Neal's place? Well, just reading it over, and there is one awkward sentence. On page 3, middle of the page: "The other thin, intense, reflecting unmistakeably qualities loosely covered by the term "intellectual", at the same time with the look of a tormented, trapped animal." That's the way it is now. "Loosely" is out to begin with. Might cut it down to this: "The other thin, intense, with the look of a tormented trapped animal." So it *reads* better, but a basic split in Bill's character has been omitted. How about: "The other thin, intense, unmistakeably intellectual, at the same time" and so forth.

Which of these alternatives do you favor? If you get around to sending it out anywhere before I get to Frisco, use your judgment. In any case "loosely" must go. With this correction, I think the story comes as near to being perfect and finished as anything I have done. What do you think?

The term "intellectual", without qualification of some sort, is in disrepute.

Well I will be glad enough to leave Tanger. The place is a huge whorehouse, and that's depressing after a while. If I had my health, and no habit, I would certainly enjoy an occasional visit here. For sex I doubt if there is anything to equal it in these barbarous times.

Love,
Bill

Making lists of things I have to do before leaving. Sure to forget something. I leave Monday and spend the night in Gibraltar. Still got habit. Will try to kick on the boat. It is too risky try bringing anything into the U.S. The chances are there would be no trouble, but if any one did spot me as a junky and they found something, I would go to prison for sure.

More Love,
Bill

Since Huxley's book on Peyote seems to have attracted attention, perhaps we could do something with the Yage material. I mean just a selection from the S.A. letters on Yage. How about *New Directions*?

I am looking forward to seeing you. You can expect me in about a month. Expect Jack to meet me at the pier with communications from you.

More Love,
Bill

30.
Sept. 3 [1954]
[Tanger]

Dear Allen,

Enclose $10. Write me full details of your financial condition. I will help you as much as I can.

What is your present status as regards Neal? He does not really intend to abide by Caroline's edict forbidding him to see you? If so he isn't the man I thought. No one should let anyone tell them who to see. Why do American males stand still for routines like this? I never did. Well Caroline has it now, what every one of them wants: a man all to herself in a suburban house full of gadgets with no pernicious friends hanging about.

Another novel opening: "Lee sat with the needle and syringe poised in his left hand, pondering the mystery of blood. Certain veins he could hit at 2:30 in the afternoon. Others were morning veins, night veins, or sometime veins that seemed to appear and disappear. Lee found his hunches were seldom wrong. That is, if he picked up the syringe with his right hand, it meant try the left arm. His body knew what vein could be hit. He let the body have its head, as in automatic writing, when he was preparing to take a shot."

I am still working on the Last Supper. So far have not hit any artesian wells of inspiration. Some good self-pity (as you know I claim the right to feel sorry for myself as a suffering human creature. What is wrong with bad self-pity is the hermetic, incestuous, luxurious wallowing in it, and above all the pitier's *refusal of insight*. On the other hand good self-pity only occurs in moments of deep insight when you see yourself clear and undistorted like a telescoped image coming into focus. You can alternatively hate yourself in these moments of revelation, but in hating yourself you hate the human race in your own image. So is self-pity, as I conceive it, wrong, sloppy and disgusting? I hope not.)—But the state like automatic writing I am in when I do my best work has not manifested itself, and I am not satisfied. Will pick up on weed and see if I can't do something with it.

What were your two pages in *Invisible Man*? I like the part about Rhinehart, and some of the scenes with the rich philanthropist in the first part. *Flee the Angry Strangers* has a few good scenes like when Ritchie—"Izzi The Ghost"—is trying to score with fuzz money and the whole Village fleeing before him. I also dug some of the pictures of underground girls. But on the whole heavy, and padded with great wads of dullness. God what a bore is that Liberal who ends up in Union Work, not to mention that athletic fighting liberal, and Stoney. There is a Signet paper book called *The Execution of Private Slovik* by someone named William Bradford Huie. Read it. Slovik was only soldier in World War II to be executed for desertion in face of the enemy. 49 others were sentenced to be shot (deserters are shot, not hanged like solders convicted of rape or murder), but none of the other sentences were carried out. Real point of the book, which the author does not make, is that Slovik was shot for telling the truth: "I would run away again". Generals are nourished on bull shit. It's their natural food. Slovik refused to give it to them—an existentialist martyr. Very much like *The Stranger* of Camus. All this is implicit. The author has no talent and no insight.

Well I want to Oh God the typewriter is going again. I want to get your $10 in the mail. The only thing nicer to see in a letter than money is a little packet of the Substance.

Love,
Bill

P.S. My illness blew over, for the present. But it will be back. I can feel it lurking about . . .

31.
Oct. 12, 1954
Palm Beach

Dear Allen

Back in Palm Beach. No bed for me in the house. I am lodged in hotel temporarily. General feeling is I should move on rather soon. "You probably won't *want* to stay more than 2 weeks" and even "Why did you come back here?"

Practical setup *very bad.* I don't have $200 per month any more. Maybe not even half that. House is mortgaged. Shop is mortgaged. I can look forward to a future of dwindling resources. Don't know what to do I am virtually unemployable under present setup, unless they are taking anybody—which they aren't now. See no immediate prospect of selling any of my literary produce.

One thing is clear. It is utterly out of the question for me to come to Frisco now unless I am 100% sure of a job. Here I am offering you aid and shelter and it looks like I have none to give.

I never felt more completely beat. Will try to make my way back to Tanger if I can raise the money.

Just as I was leaving N.Y. on my way to the airport, I ran into Solomon. Completely mad. Been supporting himself as a Good Humor man, and sold more ice cream than any other salesman in his area. He thinks his family is planning to kill him because he didn't turn out well etc. etc.

"There was more foolery yet if I could remember it."
Please write.

Love,
Bll

202 Sanford, Palm Beach. Will be here 2 weeks in any case.

32.

COBBLE STONE GARDENS

Laura Lee Burroughs   Mortimer Burroughs
231 Phipps Plaza   Palm Beach, Florida

Oct. 13 [1954]

Dear Allen,

Setup looks worse all the time. Doubtful if I can raise return fare to Tanger. They keep asking me why the Hell I came back to U.S. in the first place.

Well maybe *you* have some suggestions as to what I should do now. Only thing I can think of is to go in the Business with Ritchie or start boosting. It isn't just I don't want to work. There aren't any jobs I can get. Well I will look anyway. Maybe I can blackmail them into sending me back to Tanger. They don't want me sitting around Palm Beach, that's for sure, and the hotel (they insist no room in the house, my bed having been removed to make way for a television set) is $5 per day. Well, *a ver*. But not to mince words I *did* come back to U.S. to see you. Just wanted to put you in cognizance of my generally altered situation like I can't be shifting around any more.

Don't mean to come on sour, but this is a beat setup,

Love,
Bill

33.

[Beginning of letter missing. Letter may be out of sequence.]

Wednesday Night

Operation completed. Ritchie was supposed to show

with supplies at noon. He didn't show. I have never
suffered anything to compare with the next six hours.
Finally rolling around biting the bed and beating on the
wall, and so wrung a shot of demerol out of the nurse. I
don't know what I would have done without a shot. It was
literally intolerable. Then Ritchie shows. So I was cheated
out of the fix of a lifetime, it would have been pure relief.
Instead I am half fixed with demerol, and miss a vein, so
I don't feel the fix as much, but I am fixed now. Jack was
supposed to be here, but he hasn't showed. I must get out
of here tomorrow no matter what. This looks like the
worst infestation of the Chinaman I ever contracted.
Milwaukee and all Wisc. is legalizing junkies. They get a
permit like Mexico. I hope this splendid idea spreads. If
I could only buy codeineetas kicking would be a cinch.
But here you buy H or nothing. No dollies around
anymore. The Feds have cracked down on the dolly
writers. Georgia and Walter had some dollies to kick with,
and the Feds came and confiscated them. They don't
want anyone to kick. I will go to Florida and the family
doctor will give me a cure. Be in Frisco in 2–3 weeks.
Couldn't hurry it much anyway as I must live very quietly
until the operation heals. It would be nowhere for you to
have a semi-invalid around.

Thursday Night

Out of the hospital. Jack didn't show or call so I can
only contact him now by mail. Sometimes he seems to
lack ordinary ego-orienting sense. It wouldn't *occur* to
him to call the hospital (I had a phone in my room). I got
the nurses pretty well trained before I left, and they
brought me demerol without argument, having seen my
horrible and completely genuine exhibition of bed biting.

I still read your letter over from time to time. Went to
bed somehow knowing that I would have a Dream. Woke
up about 3 o'clock and took a small shot. Woke up now
at 7. Tremendous dream. I will write it down here: I have

returned to North Africa *several years ago—* Meet a fatuous fairy who pounces on every word with obscene double *entendre.* Beneath this camp I feel incredible evil. He clings to me, moves into a house with me. I feel sick like some loathsome insect was clinging to my body. In the street we meet two Lesbians who say "Hello Boys" recognizing Fairy-Lesbian status. A horrible, dead, ritual greeting from which I turn in retching disgust. (This perfect for ballet.) The Fairy gives me my mail he picked up at the Embassy. *Every letter has been opened,* and they are all jumbled together, typewritten pages, so *I can't tell whose letter it is.* I keep shuffling the pages looking for *the end of the letter* and a signature. I never find it.

I walk out along a dry, white road. There is danger here. A dry, brown vibrating in the air, like insect wings rubbing together. I pass a village of people sleeping, living under mounds—about 2 feet high—of black cloth stitched on wire frames. I am back in the town. The vibrating is everywhere now—horrible, dry, lifeless. Not a *sound* exactly; a *frequency,* a wave length.

The vibrating comes from a tower-like structure. A Holy Man is causing it. He has a black face. He demands more money from the townspeople. His opponents are two Arabs, the only people I have seen who look alive. One is a vigorous man in his forties, the other a boy. I am immediately attracted to the boy. I approach them and ask "How much will you give me to kill the Holy Man?" We haggle about price, but both know money is not the point. I am bragging foolishly to the boy of my marksmanship, and "I don't mind using a knife either." He looks at me and laughs, *understanding everything.* They give me a note to a gun store where I will be issued a rifle. I start into the town. A friend comes with me. He says the Holy Man is *right,* we must *accept him.* I am about to tell him about the gun, but say instead "I won't tell you any of my plans."

He says "No don't tell me. I would tell *him. You little*

fool! He knows about your silly plan!!" He shouts this with great passion, seizing my arm—"Can't I make you understand it's hopeless!"

"That—" (I am about to say the gun plan and check myself.) "is only camp. My real plan he doesn't know because I don't know it yet. *It's life*! *He* can't predict Life. only death."

"He can predict it."

"You're wrong! Wrong! I don't want to see you again for all eternity!"

I run into the town and hide from the friend in a florist shop under a case of flowers. He comes and stands there like at my coffin, wringing his hands and crying and begging me to give up the idea. I am crying too, the tears falling into dry yellow dust. But I won't give up.

Will attempt to enlarge on this dream. May provide frame work for novel. The friend, so far as I can recall, was R.W., who I haven't seen in years; a converted Catholic. He owes me $10 which I could use—well that indicates—I was thinking yesterday I could use that $10 I sent you—the friend is you too. Funny I thought it *wasn't* you at all, but Rex, and the first thing I think of is the $10. In the dream the friend looked like Rex who disappeared ten years ago. I have heard he is living in Japan, having *left his money to Mrs. K.*, John K.'s mother who has plenty money of her own. Well, want to mail this,

Love,
Bill

Write me: 202 Sanford Ave., Palm Beach, Florida

34.
Oct. 13, 1954
Palm Beach

Dear Allen,

The setup comes down to this. I can't be shifting around any more the way money is so short. I have to go someplace and plan to *stay* there. Looks like Tanger is good a place as any. It's cheap and I have Kiki.

You dig how impossible Frisco is as a permanent setup for me. If you were alone and we could live together, I would take the chance to make it there. As things are it looks more out of the question all the time from every angle. I sure made a mistake to come back to U.S. at all. Well no use to think about that. Now I want to get back there as soon as possible. Nothing for me here.

You and everybody thinks of me as coming and going as I please, like a trip to Frisco would make no difference to me one way or the other. Well the situation is changed now. I have a choice of going to Frisco or going back to Tanger, where I have Kiki and cheap living. I really can't make it in U.S. anymore. Only in N.Y., which is something special and not pure U.S.; and where I have all my junkie connections. If I ever had to turn to some illegal way of making it, N.Y. is the only place for me. Remember my position is *basically different* from yours. I am over 40. I have no work record. I am virtually unemployable except in take-anything jobs. For me to get a good, well-paying white-collar job like you have now is almost impossible. Where are my references? What have I been doing the last 20 years? I am (they think) too old for any job where I have to learn anything (for that they want college grads under 30), and I don't have the 10 to 15 years experience to take over the type of job I should normally (according to their norm) be looking for. Of course I can fake to some extent, but they are going to check. This is a worldwide Depression. Jobs are scarcer and there is sharp competition. Well just wanted to set you straight on the $ setup. Like I say, Frisco seems to me to be as out of the question for me as it would be for you to drop everything and come with me to Tanger, paying your own way. *Please let me know what you think. I have not yet made a final decision pending I hear from you.*

                Love,
                  Bill

35.
Oct. 15, 1954
[Palm Beach]

Dear Allen,

Sorry to have come on so querulous in last letter. Setup here beat beyond description. I got no trust fund. I got nothing but what they want to and can give me. Personally I see no reason why they should give me dollar one.

I saw M. in Miami. Helped him compose some job letters: "I am a young man of clean habits. I don't juice and I don't mainline" etc. sort of letters. Sent out some myself. If I get a job in Miami will hang around there awhile. Maybe M. and I will go to N.Y., and work there or go in The Business. One load of dollies back from Tanger would net $1000–$2000. Might could sell it all to Garver or Sargeant. Better than that shambles in the Village.

M. has some friends in L.A. He hears nothing good about the Coast. As you see my first concern now is to make it financial, and Frisco looks more out every time I think about it, from every angle.

                Love,
                  Bill

P.S. My friend Jimmy B. was here teaching at the Gahm-Ehes school. An ultraexpensive fashionable private joint. He was summarily fired for continual drunkenness at The Everglades Club. Too bad. This complete isolation with censorious parents and kicking interminable dolly habit is really too much. If I could only get drunk. M. sends you his love . . .

36.
Friday
Oct 29 '54
[Palm Beach]

Dear Allen,

Just received yours of Tuesday Oct. 26. Previous letter seemingly lost, as this is first letter I have from you since leaving N.Y. 3 weeks ago.

Past three weeks indescribable nightmare of junk sickness; and not over yet. I keep getting more codeine from the Doc here. New script today. I was two days without anything and couldn't make it. Prospect of final step into junkless state sets up horrible subjective reaction, a cellular panic like a fear of suffocating in unfamiliar medium. But I am going to kick, and to that end will stay here another two weeks or so until I function *sans* junk. After that I will, in all likelihood, head back to Tanger. I can live on $100 per month there and save money, which is a better deal than trying to work under current conditions. M. can't even get a job. Well I haven't decided anything definite. First thing is to kick habit.

I haven't written anything since leaving Tanger. Everything I have written reads like notes for a novel,

fragments. The final effort of creation, the novel itself, I can't achieve. I can't force it, and it won't come to me.
Please write.

Love,
Bill

P.S. Read very good novel by Italian writer. *The Dead Boy and the Comets* by Goffredo Parise.

37.
Palm Beach
202 Sanford Ave.
Nov. 8, 1954

Dear Allen,

Plan tentatively to sail Nov. 20. Still horribly sick. I went all last week without anything, then picked up a little P.G. over weekend with Betty. I feel awful today, but I felt worse Friday so maybe the P.G. didn't make any difference.

Like I wrote about a week ago, I have only received one letter from you since I am here. The letter about movie idea I never got. Are you sure you mailed it? Kells is back in Mexico. I had a letter from Alan Ansen he was thrown out of his apartment for immoral conduct. In fact his status in Italy is dubious.

Please write to me.

Love,
Bill

38.
Palm Beach
Nov. 12, '54
202 Sanford Ave.
Friday

Dear Allen,

Thanks for letter. I am still suffering from P.G. weekend with Betty. Never knew anything to hang on like this. Never again will I kick on the street.

Scheduled to sail Sat. Nov. 20. Sorry I can't meet you in N.Y. Another month here would unseat my reason.

Been reading everything I can find on the Amazon. I am convinced The Lost Inca City is a fact. Independent accounts place it in some approximate area (where Fawcett disappeared and still most dangerous spot in the Amazon Basin. Hostile Indians etc.). Seemingly it was inhabited by light-skinned Inca descendants in 1900, is probably empty now, but loaded with gold. As soon as I can save the $ I am going to have a look.

Sure I am agreeable to make any changes in Ms. However I am exceedingly uncreative just now on account of my junk trouble. What a relief it will be to get back to Tanger. If you shift to N.Y. I will be seeing you soon, either in N.Y. or Europe. Everything you tell me about Frisco sounds like U.S. Inferno. Have you dug Brubeck etc., new telepathic jazz? I didn't realize till this past month how awful America is. God what a fate to live here! (N.Y., of course, is not America.)

I heard from Alan. He was caught by a servant *in flagrante* and thrown out of his apartment. Italy still sounds like a bad deal to me. Address is c/o American Express, Venice, Italy.

Will be curious to hear what Rexroth says.

Sat.

Still sick. If I was anywhere else could taper off with codeine or demerol. But I have already burned the town down on P.G.

If you run into anybody wants to look for The Lost City and all that Inca gold, and can put up a few thousand $, let me know.

Love,
Bill

39.
Dec. 6, '54
Tanger

Dear Allen,

Back in the promised land: Been spending 15–20 hours every day in bed with Kiki. I don't realize what a drag the U.S. can be, until I hit a free county and get relief in every direction.

You are, of course, authorized to make any alteration, deletions etc. you see fit in my Ms. What does Rexroth mean by his remarks on the Roosevelt skit: "by one who had no touch with the higher ups"? It's not supposed to be *accurate*. Does he think it has anything to do with *Roosevelt*? His remarks seem to me completely inapplicable.

I sat down seriously to write a best seller, and the result is another routine. I will send it along when I can latch onto a typewriter. At present I don't have one and no money to buy even a second-hand machine. I am really beat for bread.

I am discouraged about my writing. It seems impossible for me to write anything saleable, or, in fact, anything that achieves artistic unity or wholeness. What I have written reads like the notes for a novel, not the novel itself. The act of creation needed to unify material into a finished work, seems beyond my power. All I can write is pieces of a novel, and the pieces don't fit together.

I finally paid Jack the $30. My financial state is deplorable. I should pull myself together and write something. Write me c/o U.S. Legation, Tanger.

Love,
Bill

P.S. Started taking Eukodol when I hit town. Now I must stop. The stuff paralyzes my bladder so I can't piss. Tapering off with demerol, P.G. and codeine. Besides I want to kick. All those weeks of suffering in Florida will be wasted if I get back on now. But I never had a habit hang on like this. I had nothing on the boat, and was sick the whole week with no relief in sight. I went to a doctor about this difficulty pissing, and he says take some coramine to counteract the junk. Fine thing, I have to take a shot of coramine every time I want to piss.

40.
Dec. 13, 1954
Tanger

Dear Allen,

I always have so much I want to say to you that a letter is a major operation. Never get it all said, either. I wish you could make it here.

I am downright incapacitated without a typewriter, but have written 1st chapter of a novel in which I will incorporate all my routines and scattered notes. Scene is Tanger, which I call Interzone. Did I write you anything about novel in progress? Starts with a deal to import and sell "a load of K.Y. made of genuine whale dreg in the South Atlantic, currently quarantined by the Board of Health in Tierra del Fuego." (Whale dreg is what remains after they get finished cooking down a whale. A rotten, stinking, fishyness you can smell for miles. No use has been found for it.)

As you gather, in my most extreme line. I am going to attempt to complete work. I am afraid it will be as unpublishable as *"costumbre"*. Did I tell you about my Merchant Marine papers? The application came back from Washington with a notation in civil service code, whereupon they gave me a form to fill out. "Are you or have you ever been addicted to" etc. They were very nice about it all, patting me on the shoulder. The application has to go back to Washington again. It looks hopeless.

The drug store here is packing me in. They have sold me 10 boxes to kick on, and Kiki is doling them out according to a schedule. This is a lucky break. I was compulsively taking larger doses at shorter intervals, and experiencing paranoid kicks. For example a group of Arabs walk by and I distinctly hear them say: "William Burroughs", and it seems everyone I pass in cafés is looking at me, laughing and commenting. At the same time I *experience* these hallucinations, I *know* they are paranoid reactions caused by the drug, so I am not alarmed; that is, I *know* they are not real. A curious state of simultaneous insight and hallucination.

If there is any possibility of publishing *Naked Lunch* I have some notes on cocaine that belong in it, but in the *Junk* section. I don't know as it's a good idea to drop *Junk*. (You will recall I put some of the material from *Queer* back into *Junk*.) Well, use your judgement. I am up to my neck in this new work right now, plus kicking habit. Besides I don't have a complete Ms. In fact I have hardly any of *Queer*. I still think Roosevelt skit is funny. Sounds to me like Rexroth just doesn't dig what a routine is. You don't study Zen and then write a scholarly routine, for Christ's sake! Routines are completely spontaneous and proceed from whatever fragmentary knowledge you have. In fact a routine is by nature fragmentary, inaccurate. There is no such thing as an exhaustive routine, nor does the scholarly-type mind run to routines.

Well I must close now. Must get to work on my new novel. This writing in longhand is extremely exhausting. Please write.

Love,
Bill

P.S. When I was home I fell into a disgusting state of stagnation, ate and slept to excess. A horrible thing was happening to me. I was getting *fat*. An inch of nasty soft flesh, marring my flat stomach I have always been so proud of. And I felt terrible. No energy, no life. It would literally *kill* me to live in U.S., except maybe in Frisco or N.Y. I could make it.

Now I feel alert and charged with energy, and my gut is once again hard and flat. It's like I can't breathe in the U.S., especially in suburban communities. Palm Beach is a real horror. No slums, no dirt, no poverty. God what a fate to live there! No wonder men die young in U.S. and women outlive them and batten on their insurance. The U.S. simply does not provide sustenance for a man. He gets fat, and his vitality drains away, and he dies from spiritual malnutrition. It is significant that in other cultures (like Islam, for example), men live as long or longer than women, while in U.S. statistics show women outlive men by a wide margin.

So I am counting my blessings in Tanger. Awful thought occurs to me. Suppose I am like preserved in junk and will get fat if and when I get off it? What a dilemma! I would probably sacrifice everything to my narcissism and preserve my flat stomach at any cost.

Glimpsed a new *dimension* of sex: Sex mixed with routines and laughter, the unmalicious, unstrained, *pure* laughter that accompanies a good routine, laughter that gives a moment's freedom from the cautious, nagging, aging, frightened flesh. How angelic such an affair could be! (Note that sex and laughter are considered incompatible. You are supposed to take sex seriously. Imagine a Reichian's reaction to my laughing sex kick! But it is the nature of laughter to recognize no bounds.)

So here I am way off the subject doing a mambo with Miss Green and is she ever in the slot tonight! And in this number the Rejection Dance, the Anti-Sex that mambo basically is, finds graphic representation. The man turns towards the woman with a hard-on that subsides as he digs her. The sex organs are artificial, huge, *papier-mâché* constructions. As the dance progresses they become more and more realistic, until we get to the real thing. The woman does a mocking dance showing her cunt and her ass in rapid, whirling succession as if to say "It's all one to you the Eternal Pederast." He polishes his nails on his erection in parody of sulky male indifference, etc.

Infinite possibilities. A tremendous Ballet of Rejection, Desecration and Repression of Life. If successful would be unbearably depressing, unless I can produce a rebuttal. Well I will think on it. Whole idea just came to me this second.

Well Bowles has gone with all his retinue. I do wish I had somebody to *talk* to.

41.
Dec. 28 - '54
[Tanger]

Dear Allen,

Just received your letter. Sounds great and I will do my best to get material in order. Right off hand I don't know of too many changes to be made in the S.A. letters, except for finishing up the Yage City section, and throwing out some of those diseased beggars. Remember I have already spent five months in N.Y. just in working over the letters. Well I will see.

What to do about habit is my number one problem. In Florida I took two-week reduction under supervision of a croaker. Then one month with nothing but about the equivalent of four bottles codeine cough syrup, which is to say nothing. At the end of the month I was still sick, but like I was never sick before. That is I can eat and sleep all right but no strength in my muscles, no alertness in my body. And most horrible of all, I was getting fat. Not being as narcissistic as I am, you can not realize the feeling of cold horror with which I saw this inch of flab accumulating inexorably around my stomach. I was two days in N.Y. and split a skimpy five-cent bag with Stanley Gould. A tremendous wave of euphoria and relief swept over me. A host of disagreeable subjective manifestations which I thought had no connection with withdrawal were gone. One more shot in N.Y, then eight-day trip with nothing and reached Tanger sick. So I am hooked again. I feel alert, tireless, and my stomach is once again hard and flat. In short the picture has changed. I never tried to kick a habit that hung on like this. And this fat is something new. The question is, can I make it without junk? I'd like to try without for a year or so. But I don't propose to be half–alive, and I don't intend to get fat either. Perhaps junk suspends the aging process in some sinister way; as I get older I will age hideously between shots, ever larger doses being necessary to save my body from the encroaching flab. Well enough about my metabolic processes. Kiki is taking a trip to Melilla next week, and I intend to sample some of the local cous cous (that's an Arab dish).

I have written a short story. I will send it along in another envelope. I don't think much of it, but I may be wrong. Anyway have a look at it. If it's as bad as I think it is, throw it away. Now as to the Roosevelt skit and similar material, all I can do is to include in the Ms. what I think is good. Judgment as to whether it is too much, too wild, I can't make—especially not as regards my own work. You do that, and I will accept your judgments. Yes I have a copy of the S.A. letters, complete except for the bar part at the end of the City. Please send along a copy of that.

I am planning to write, when I get the time, a short book just on Yage like Huxley's peyote book. Positively no school–boy smut. No purple-assed baboons, no prolapsed ass holes, by God not even any piles, no gags like: "Gus," I said quietly, trying to keep my voice steady, "We're out of K.Y." What I mean is, Al, I'm going to keep it clean.

Kiki has moved in with me. I would like to find a place with more room so he could have a bed of his own and some place to stash his gear. I don't want him sleeping with me every night. He is looking for a furnished house. We had one lined up: four rooms and bath, fully and well furnished in Native Quarter for $23 a per month. But the owner was afraid to antagonize my landlord, Tony, because Tony is such a potent pimp. The queens are all afraid to cross him lest he cut off their supply of boys. They also think he has an in with the law because an old auntie fuzz man gets his boys through Tony, and Tony always has some garbled story about what is going on at Headquarters.

Alan Ansen is still loving Venice. He plans to visit me in March. There was something very unpleasant about N.Y. this last time. Like everybody off their rocker. A nasty, metallic hysteria. Everybody half on the junk. Jack was in his best form of unconscious sabotage, inviting extra people to come along and take a shot with me, people I never see before. I got on the boat with nothing. A junk-sick boat trip is like pure time. I did some phenomenal sleeping, but boredom pursued me even in sleep.

Well I will get started on the S.A. letters. I will also type up and send along first chapter of my current novel.

Rereading your letter. By all means send me copy of Yage City and Bar section and I will finish it. For God's sake don't waste time in Chicago. It's really nowhere at all.

                Love,
                 Bill

               42.
            Dec. 30, '54
             [Tanger]

Dear Allen,

Here is that short story. I don't think much of it, but got writing on it and couldn't stop. As matter of fact I feel deeply discouraged about my writing at present. I will start typing up the novel now, and send along chapter by chapter.

No news around here.

                Love,
                 Bill

P.S.   The story is sloppily written in places, and I could improve on it or rather smooth it out if you think it's worth bothering with at all.

               43.
            Dec. 30, 1954
             [Tanger]

Dear Allen,

Enclose first chapter of current novel. Reading it over, I get an impression of something very sinister just under the surface, but I don't know what it is. Just a feeling. The second chapter covers some material I wrote before, some of which you must have seen. From there on I have no plans. Will let the book write itself.

I will work over the S.A. letters, and let you know about alterations. Suspending work on novel to give all my time to the letters. The magazine sounds great. I only hope nothing fucks it up. You can count on me to help out any way possible.

Love,
Bill

P.S. What's this about Rexroth saying Auden says Jack is a genius but ruined by his friends? Jack wrote me that. Also Auden says I am a genius too.

Jack sounds paranoid. The cops caught up with him and served non-support warrant. He says he has imitators in Frisco, owing to your lack of discretion. What's this about you have a boy in Frisco?

44.
Jan. 12, 1955
Tanger

Dear Allen,

I think I am at the point of jumping in the lake instead of skirting the edges, and feel a great need for your help at this critical juncture. In fact I think we might even be able to collaborate on this novel.

Here is from the blurb jacket of the novel. Getting a bit previous, I admit. The theme just came to me in the form of this blurb:

"Suppose you knew the power to start an atomic war

lay in the hands of a few scientists who were bent on destroying the world? That is the terrifying question posed by this searching novel."

"The book grabs you by the throat." Says L. Marland, distinguished critic. "It leaps in bed with you and performs unmentionable acts. Then it thrusts a long cold needle deep into your spine and gives you an injection of ice water. That is the only way I know to express the feeling of fear that reaches out of these pages. Behind the humor, the routines, the parody (some of it a bit heavy-handed to be sure), you glimpse a dead-end despair, a bleak landscape of rubble under the spreading black cloud of a final bomb.

"The desperate struggle of a handful of men with the forces and emissaries of Destruction has the immediacy of a barroom fight, the kick to the groin, the broken beer bottle thrust at the eye.

"This book is a must for anyone who would understand the sick soul, sick unto death, of the atomic age."

So that's the novel of which I sent you the first chapter . . . I can work in all my routines, all the material I have written so far on Tanger that is scattered through a hundred letters to you.

When I don't have inspiration for the novel I busy myself with hack work. I am writing an article on Tanger. Perhaps *New Yorker:* "Letter from Tanger". Will send along in a few days. You should be able to sell it. After that will write an article on Yage, possibly a short book with photos. I have some very fine pictures of me and the Yage vine taken by Doc Schultes. He sent me these photos when I was in Florida. I wrote a thank-you letter and sent a specimen of the plant used to potentiate Yage that I collected in Peru (hiterto the other ingredients *were not known* so it is a matter of some importance) for the collection at the Harvard Botanical Museum. He was a great help to me, and a very nice person.

You should have all the Yage corrections now except the final version and end to the Yage City and Bar section. Please keep me posted constantly. Sometimes I wish I had come to Frisco.

Love,
Bill

45.
No idea what the date is
(Jan 21, '55
Tanger . . . A.G.)

Dear Allen,
　The typewriter is fucked again, and so far to carry it to be fixed—it is heavy desk model.
　I am suffering from a profound depression, the worst of my life. I have a complete conviction that I can't write any more—that my talent, such as it is, has given out—and sit for hours looking at a blank page. And there is no one I can talk to. I shouldn't be here hung up on Eukodol. Of course take more, on account of depression. I should have gone to Frisco.
　I don't know what is wrong with me, but it is bad. Every idea I get on my novel seems ridiculous, like this atomic deal. And everything I write disgusts me. Some fucking German came here and committed suicide, so now it's RX for everything even goof balls . . . such a bore. The druggist goes out and gets my script while I wait.
　There was a Danish boy around town a few weeks ago. He was here last year and ran out of money and I helped him out, but this time I figure it's too much. And such a dreary "déjà vu"—exactly the same setup. So I tell him "Go get yourself repatriated," so the Danish Consul sends him home on a Danish ship which sank with all hands in the North Sea. Don't know why I mention it. It's very

uninteresting. He gave me an alarm clock, just before he went away, which keeps very poor (not even appropriate) time. The other mooch preyed on me last year, the Portuguese, is rumored to be dead too, of unknown causes in Madrid.

I really feel *awful*. A feeling of complete desolation. This typewriter is impossible.

Love,
Bill

P.S. I did not receive copy of Yage City section. Have had no word from you in the past 3 weeks or so.

Just looking over what I wrote last night. It is terrible. I wrote an article on Tanger but it depresses me to see it even. It is so flatly an *article* like anybody could have written. I will send it along, however, when I get around to making a few corrections. Maybe you can sell it someplace. I don't know.

46.
Feb. 19, '55
Tanger

Dear Allen,

Heartfelt thanks for the check, which arrived dramatically as the Embassy was closing its doors, and saved my camera. That morning Alan Ansen had surprised me most agreeably by sending a check for 5000 lira—about $15. (I had mentioned my financial condition but had not asked, or even hinted, that he send me anything.) Imagine the shock of disappointment—(6 cents, 2 shots, and half a loaf of stale bread constituted my total assets)—when the bank told me this type check is only negotiable in Italy. I tried to borrow money. Those that would lend it don't have any, and those that have won't lend. Not centavo one could I promote. My only recourse is to sell the camera. I take it to a Hindu shopkeeper who says "Come back in two hours and I will give you my price." He won't do business on the spot. So I rush to Embassy on the chance of letter from you, and there is your check. Jerk my camera back from disgruntled Hindu.

I am living now on strict budget and should be able to avoid such acute crisisi (plural of crisis) in future. I was able to cash that personal check because I have a friend with a bank account. Otherwise I would have to wait weeks for it to clear. Money can also be sent by American Express checks made out to me. American Express could explain this method. Cost is nominal. International money order takes about 3 weeks to clear. So either personal checks or American Express is best method. American Express preferable if not too much trouble, as this friend might renege on cashing checks for me.

The novel is taking shape. Something even more evil than atomic destruction is the theme—namely an anti-dream drug which destroys the symbolizing, myth-making, intuitive, empathizing, telepathic faculty in man, so that his behavior can be controlled and predicted by the scientific methods that have proved so useful in the physical sciences. In short, this drug eliminates the disturbing factor of spontaneous, unpredictable life from the human equation. I have spoken of the increased sensitivity to dream-like, nostalgic impressions that is conveyed by light junk-sickness. This is point of departure for creation of anti-dream drug. Novel treats of vast Kafkian conspiracies, malevolent telepathic broadcast stations, the basic conflict between the East—representing spontaneous, emergent life—and the West, representing control from without, character armor, death. But it is difficult to know what side anyone is working on, especially yourself. Agents continually infiltrate to work on other side and discredit by excesses of zeal; more accurately, agents rarely know which side they are working on.

At the same time Scientists are working on the anti-dream drug, dream situations are breaking through into three-dimensional reality, and drugs have been discovered to increase symbolizing and telepathic powers so that any deviant threatens The Controllers, who seemingly have every advantage since they have precisely the means of Control on three-dimensional level (Police, armies, atom bombs, poison gas etc.), but this great mass of armor suffocates them like over-armored dinosaurs—(however, the outcome is left in doubt).

I wasn't using the right approach? So that's it! Well that can be remedied. I will eat wheat germ oil, exercise and think Positive Thoughts until I crackle with vigor, leaving a faint odor of ozone in my wake against backdrop of romantic adventure. Unfortunately, in our culture, adventure is almost synonomous with crime; hence fantasies of committing crime for loved one. South America offers adventure without crime, hence my desire to make expedition with you.

Your boy was indeed traumatized. At what age did this occur? Did he remember it or was memory brought out in analysis? Is he really satisfied now with chicks? You said he was 22? That seems late to be *discovering* the cunt. Why can't you take a photo of him? You have that 35 mm camera, do you not?

I appreciate your critical notes on my work. They have been very helpful to me. I guess all writers suffer from fear of losing their talent, because talent is something that seems to come from outside, that you have no control over.

Too bad the magazine deal fell through.

There is a hip American bullfighter in town name of Tuck Porter. Nice stud. He made pod but not junk. Knows Stanley Gould. Spent 3 years in Mexico. Also met woman who was in Peru and knows about Yage (but never tried it).

When I get next month's allowance I will try to buy a typewriter. A new portable here costs $50. Second-hand machines run $25–$35. I am pretty well in the clear now. Haven't run up any debts this month. Next few days will be pretty lean, but I'll make it. Must close now and get this in the mail. Thanks again for life-saving check.

Love,
Bill

P.S. Glad you liked the story. I will send along article when I get typewriter.

47.
March 15, 1955
Tanger

Dear Allen,

It is a long time since I heard from you. You received my letter thanking you for check?

Alan Ansen is here, and enjoying himself immensely with a different boy every night. Venice doesn't sound like such a great place to me.

I am running out of money again. O connections unreliable, and no saving. I must either quit or cut down drastically, but do not want to be out of action during Alan's visit. If you could send me some more money I would certainly appreciate it, even $5 or $10, as I will be flat broke in another week and Alan will probably need all his money to get back to Venice.

I have been working, handicapped by lack of typewriter. I have that article about ready, and also a story about my young friend who was killed by a lion in a border town nightclub. I will send along when I get typed. Have you heard anything from Jack? I haven't heard from him in months. Dreamed I was defending him against attacking Negroes in a deserted sawmill.

Enclose 2 pictures of me, one of which shows the depression and sadness I suffer from lately. Please let me hear from you. Alan sends his love.

Love,
Bill

Can only find one photo. Not the depressed one.

I have my own house now. Can't get up energy to clean it, and live here in slowly accumulating dirt and disorder.

Maybe I will feel a little better when I get my shotgun and kill something. It has taken me all this while to get a permit.

48.
March 31, '55
Tanger

Dear Allen,

Letters continue criss cross. Received yours today after sent one out to you.

The pictures of M. very good but rather pitiless. Every mole shows. And there is one appalling picture of me, looking fattish with sagging breasts and petulant old queen expression.

Keep me posted on Neal. "Battling the radiations of time, against the stream, slowly eaten away" is very good line of poetry.

Alternate friendly and stand-offish come-on is a basic pattern with W. He came on exactly like that with me. I can't figure whether he suspects everyone of designs on his person which he must nip in distasteful bud, but decided finally it was automatic basic reaction in all his interpersonal relations. He needs analysis (Incidentally he doesn't approve of analysis: "All analysts are peeping Toms.").

I met an interesting Harvard man, or rather Alan met him first, who is here on Ford Foundation doing a history of Morocco. Fantastically brilliant linguist—Japanese, Russian, Czechoslovakian, Arabic, and of course all the European languages. He says Arab literature and notably the Koran is very great. They have a special mood-tense to express intense religious experience. I have been studying a spot of Arabic but despair of learning to read it. Just figure to pick up a few words for conversation purposes.

I have been making the rounds of the good restaurants here with Alan, and the prices really are fantastic. First-class French restaurant, snails *à la Bourgogne*, chicken cooked in wine and delicious lima beans, a terrific chocolate frozen *mousse*, Camembert cheese, fruit—all for $1, and there are about 6 or 8 restaurants in this price range and excellence. Meals would cost $5 in U.S. Tanger really is a comfortable and convenient place to live, no doubt about that.

Yes I tried Thorazine for junk sickness, and it didn't do me too much good, but I was taking it orally. Injected in a schedule with some barbiturates I can see how it might be highly effective. It does make one sleep. They are also using reserpine for withdrawal. I tried that and found it nowhere. Thorazine is better. Reserpine is Indian snakeroot used by Gardi. Very effective in calming disturbed schizophrenics, and depressed cases. So far as withdrawal goes, we are still waiting for the wonder drug that will knock out the symptoms without being a substitute habit-forming narcotic like dolophine or demerol.

International set up looks real bad; China obviously wants war, and it only takes one to start a war. Well *in'ch'Allah* (as Allah wills).

A *new* Swiss portable typewriter is $50 here. No use

bothering with second-hand desk models—no used portables around at $30. This is cheap place to buy a typewriter. I am trying to promote one on installments.

Love,
Bill

Do you know Jack's address? He just said he was South, fugitive from wife I presume. Willy Gaddis's book is out. I saw reviews in *Newsweek*.

49.
March 31, 1955
Tanger

Dear Allen,

Thanks for your checks and the photos. Returning Mexican photos of you as per instructions.

Just saw Alan Ansen off. He was here almost a month and apparently had a most enjoyable *séjour*. A boy almost every day, and expressed amazement at the excellent cuisine and reasonable prices of Tanger. There are a number of *very good* French restaurants in this town where you can eat an entire dinner from snails to camembert for $1. In fact I doubt if there is any town anywhere with such excellent food for so little money. Alan also says the boy situation is much easier and pleasanter than Venice, and all prices drastically less. All in all I gathered no very good impression of Venice as place of abode.

I am still hamstrung without a typewriter, but hope for a royalty check. I have ready to type an article on Tanger, a short story about my friend who was killed by a lion in border town nightclub, an article with photos on Yage. All this material should be saleable. I plan to make next

6 months a test as to whether I can make an approximation of a living from writing—by that time I should have a novel in shape, in addition to various short pieces. If I can't make it writing, plan to imigrate to S.A., probably Peru, with idea of making a living there. You see I don't have any trust fund. My $200 per month is a straight allowance realized from the shop. I face a future of dwindling income, and must make provision. If necessary I can always live in jungle for almost nothing. Of course I am going to see Europe and probably the Near East before returning. If any money forthcoming *may* see Far East with particular attention to Bangkok (Siam) and Japan. (Tentative plan to buy sizeable quantity of H, and return U.S. via S.A. or Mexico. A few pieces would straighten out my financial difficulties. Well, that's all quite tentative.).

Point is I must think of future and evolve definite plan. Right now intend to give all my attention and time to writing as soon as I can latch onto a typewriter.

No, I doubt if you could make any time with E. W. (he's too fat for me). When I knew him he was active with chicks. What's wrong with him now? How is your boy Peter? Hell, give me Kiki or Angelo and fuck all these complications. Neal's third ball is undoubtedly a rupture, and should be operated *without delay* or will get worse and may strangulate. Urge him to seek out a competent M.D. *at once.*

I have been taking cure or at least cutting down, with Kiki doling out the ampules. My God these immature Americans! Imagine a boy of 22 not yet knowing whether he's really satisfied with chicks—(Just reading your letter again) and not satisfied with men either. Like I say God deliver me from these American hassles.

Hope to be able to send along the material I have ready to type in another week or so. Everything hinges on a royalty check. Otherwise no typewriter this month, unless I can get one on the installment plan.

I cannot make it in U.S. so far as jobs go if I have to

go to work. There simply are no Stateside jobs I could get or would be able to endure. So if I have to work, will choose country like Peru with frontier conditions.

                Love,
                   Bill

50.
April 20 [1955]
Tanger

Dear Allen,

Miss Green always accentuates prevailing mood. Depends which way you are leaning. I'm too precarious to venture a date with her, though she's always around the house to accomodate visitors. I received $5 check for which many thanks.

Trying to kick. Seems hopeless. I didn't get back on when I came back to Tanger. I never was off. All those weeks in Florida and another week on the boat, and I hit Tanger sick. I should have gone to Lexington for the winter season. Now I have to quit or find some place where junk is cheaper—I can't control this Eukodol. Not that it's so great. It always leaves you feeling not quite fixed, like you need a little more. A shot of Eukodol is like a hot bath that isn't *quite* hot enough, if you dig me. But this not knowing where next shot is coming from—I am living on the level of an Australian Aborigine. I spend all my money on junk and don't eat right. Considering a shift to Near East, Beirut, which is said to flow with junk like the Promised Land.

Woke up last night 3 A.M. with a character in mind who is writing "a great, gloomy, soul-searing homosexual novel. Six hundred pages of heartache and loneliness and frustration." Title *Ignorant Armies* from Dover Beach:

"Swept with confused alarms of struggle and flight
Where ignorant armies clash by night."

The hero Adrian Scudder: "His face had the look of a superimposed photo, reflecting a fractured spirit that could never love man or woman with complete sincerity or wholeness, yet driven by an overwhelming passion to change fact, to make *this* love real. Usually he selected someone who could not or would not reciprocate, enabling him to shift (cautiously, like one who tests uncertain ice, though in this case the danger was not that the ice should give way, but that it might hold his weight) the burden of failure onto the partner. The recipients of his dubious affections often felt the necessity of declaring neutrality, feeling themselves surrounded by a struggle of great, dark purposes, but not in direct danger, only liable to be caught in line of fire, because basically they were outsiders. Adrian was the last of a strange archaic clan, or, perhaps, the first. In any case he was without context, of no class and no place." And that terrific last scene where Adrian puts his head in a gas oven after killing Mark, and vomits and shits (see note below) and finally tries to get out just as he is losing consciousness: "Seized with the panic of one buried alive, he tried to sit straight up through the jagged metal of the stove. Pinwheels of pain careened through his head, setting off a fresh paroxysm of nausea. He saw a high wall and a little metal door, and he knew he must somehow get through the door, get the door open and get out through the door . . . No, he had not been allowed to slip away like one who leaves a dull party early with a few negligent handshakes, and the meaning look across the room to the one he will see later, perhaps. It was as if all the incarnate demons of his cautious, aging, frightened flesh, that he had tormented so long and with such cool malice, had mustered at the door of death to pelt him with filth, trip him, and finally kick him through the door, unwilling, whimpering, soiling himself like a frightened ape."

By God, Allen, that's purple as a baboon's ass! Why do I always parody? Neither in life nor in writing can I achieve complete sincerity—like Adrian of the novel—*except* in parody and moments of profound discouragement. (Kitchen gas often causes vomiting and uncontrollable diarrhea. I recall years ago in Chicago I helped the landlady break down the door where a woman was trying to kill herself with gas. She had shit all over herself. Ray took advantage of the confusion to steal her wristwatch.)

I have introduced some new characters into the novel: A man given to surrealist puns and practical jokes. Someone asks (an Englishman, of course) for a fag (cigarette in English slang, case you don't know)—and he produces, from under a great black cloak, a screaming, swishing fruit, who goes jabbering and swishing off stage. He is in a bad restaurant (with pretensions to be good), as I was the other night and complained about the meat and they said "Oh it must be good it comes from a good butcher shop" (not *looking* at it, you dig). Faced by this contingency, my boy lets out a great cry, and in comes a *troupe* of great, filthy, snorting hogs and he feeds them his plate. (Did you ever hear anyone call hogs? They give this weird, long cry and the hogs come running and grunting with anticipation from incredible distances. The pig is by no means a stupid animal.) This character also keeps a purple-assed baboon, sometimes whipping the animal through a crowded café. (On the other hand I think I will have a blind man with a seeing-eye baboon. Which do you think is best?)

I sympathize with all your feelings of depression, beatness: "We have seen the best of our time." You at least can make a living, and perhaps a very good living. It wouldn't surprise me if you achieved a considerable degree of success in the way of a high-paying job. I'm absolutely nowhere so far as a job goes in U.S. Only hope lies in the jungles of S.A., or conceivably writing a book that will sell. Now that seems about as likely as winning the lottery. Majorca is readily accessible from here. Cost about $25. It is a nice place. I am hoarding demerol and Paracodina (Codeine tablets *à la Mexicaine*, which are available here but only sporadically. Supply is uncertain.) in a new attempt to kick. Despite new restrictions Tanger is still fantastic by U.S. standards. Imagine buying demerol in shootable ampules right across the counter. In fact the druggist called it to my attention. I am famous all over town, and the druggists bring out the best they can sell without RX when I walk in, saying: "Bueno . . . fuerto." ("Good . . . strong.") They are shameless, and always try to overcharge, but how much pleasanter than the sour, puritanical shits in U.S. drugstores. In N.Y. I had a script for codeine tablets. I give it to this old fuck and his *pince-nez* falls off. Then he calls the doctor (but can't find him in), asks questions, finally refuses to fill the script without talking to the doctor. *Codeine*!! Here plain codeine, 1/10 the U.S. price, has written on the tube: *No script necessary for sale.*

I have no companionship here since Alan went back to Venice. I told you about Charles Gallagher, who is writing a history of Morocco for Ford Foundation? Very charming, and a brilliant linguist. He says "Ghazil" can mean almost anything. Unfortunately he is gone to Rabat to be with the archives, but will return in the summer. It is really a deprivation to be without intelligent conversation. I evolve concepts, but no one to communicate with. Well enough I am getting garrulous.

Love,
Bill

51.
May 17, 1955
[Tanger]

Dear Allen,

Just back from 14-day cure in clinic. Lost 30 pounds. No junk. Knocked out on barbiturates 4 days. After that all the usual, plus a substantial case of the horrors. Still sick and sensitized to the point of hallucination. Everything looks sharp and different like it was just washed. Sensations hit like tracer bullets. I feel a great intensity building up, and at same time a weakness like I can only keep myself *here*, back now in this doughy, dead flesh I have been away from since the habit started. (Feel like I was back from years in a concentration camp.) No sex. No hunger. Just not alive yet, but feel like I never feel it before. Junk is death. I don't ever want to see it or touch it or commerce in it. Way I feel now I'd rather sell lottery tickets than touch The Business.

Curious dream last night, which I want to get down.

I was in a suicide clinic in Turkey. You just sit there and wait until you feel like it. I was sitting on a ledge overlooking bare snow-topped mountains like the Andes. A young boy (14–15) came and stood beside me. Then I could feel myself slipping further and further *out*. (The actual suicide is performed in a plane that takes you and the boy and crashes in the Pass. No one ever got through the Pass in the history of the Clinic.) As I am still slipping further and further out and the Plane is coming for me, Dave Wollman—friend here—takes my arm like he actually did last night when I started to faint in the street, and says "Stay here with us, Bill. There's plenty of time."

In the clinic you can always leave anytime before you get in the Plane. "We just give you the chance. Whether you take it or not is up to you." (I saw a bearded dope fiend hurrying to catch the boat back to the mainland. Boat whistle in distance.) You can even take your Boy out with you. Mine said: "I won't go with you unless you kick and stay kicked."

There is preparation similar to Yage used here in Morocco. This I will personally investigate when I get back my strength.

Wish you were here as I could do with some outside help. Write soon. I have long letter from Jack.

Love,
Bill

P.S.   Thanks for last $5. From here on I will be having no pressing $ worries.

May 30, 1955

P.S.   Some backsliding (codeineetas and demerol), but I am making it. This time I mean to get cured and stay cured. No joy pops. I don't want to see any more junk as long as I live.

52.
July 5, '55
Tanger

Dear Allen,

I have been too discouraged and disgusted to write. The trouble was I left the hospital half sick. Two weeks is not long enough for me to kick now. I used to kick in ten days.

Even so I probably would have made it except I came down with an excruciatingly painful neuralgia in the back. I thought I had kidney stones. I never experienced such pain. That finished me, and I relapsed into demerol which is really evil shit. After that awful cure it is really heartbreaking to find myself hooked again. . . . But I am more determined than ever to quit. Even if I have to take the whole cure over. This time I'm going to succeed. If I don't kick now I never will . . . I wish you were here. I am so disgusted with my prevaricating—always some excuse for one last box—I have been buying absolutely the last box of demerol ampules every day for the past 3 weeks. Such a dreary display of weakness. At the same time I want to be rid of junk more than I ever wanted anything. So tomorrow I will shift to codeine, and try a rapid reduction. If I don't make it I will return to the clinic. Everyone thinks it's hopeless . . . I would gladly go to jail for a month and kick cold.

Maybe I will have Kiki take my clothes away and dole out the codeineetas. But I've done that so many times before. Well I hope I can report definite success in next letter.

I have met Paul Bowles, by the way. Very nice. In fact there are quite a few people of interest around now.

I will write in more detail later on. Want to get this in the mail.

Love,
Bill

53.
July 12, '55
Tanger

Dear Allen,

I am involved in a strange Kafkian boat trip to Dakar and Freetown and back. A motor yacht carrying cargo . . . 15 days down and back. I plan to take only codeine and dispossess the Chinaman.

This trip is a typical fucked-up Tanger routine. The owners—2 Englishmen—are flat ass broke and I have been lending them money to eat on. The Captain is an old alcoholic bum who has been around Tanger as far back as anyone can remember, cadging drinks and sleeping on the street. (It's like you got on a boat and found that Joe Gould or Maxwell Bodenheim was the Captain.) The cook, with whom I share a cabin, is a confirmed hypochondriac specializing in unsavory symptoms. Right now he is in a dysentery period—Middle to Late Dysentery—and I am subject to hourly bulletins on the color and consistency of his "stool" as he calls it, coming on genteel like in a Cockney accent. Thirty days of Leslie's stool may well unseat my reason. I prescribe he should plug up his ass as a bad job and start over again someplace else, with a clean slate so to speak.

It seems that everything hinges on a cable from Freetown. On the basis of this cable they expect to borrow money from the bank. The bank stipulates as condition of the loan that we pick up in Freetown and return to Tanger an undisclosed cargo. I don't know why they refuse to reveal the content of this cargo, but it sounds ominous. I suspect something of a noxious or dangerous character.

We certainly have a cargo of Jonahs. Anything can happen on this trip. Supposedly there will be no liquor aboard. But they all plan to sneak a few bottles. May Allah grant the Captain doesn't get his hands on any. No one else has the vaguest idea of navigation.

How is your work coming along? I will commentate on your poem under separate cover. It is somewhere in an appalling mess of letters, manuscripts, receipted bills, empty demerol boxes, hypos, clothes and books. Sometimes I wish I was neater.

I have no plans. The most important thing for me now is to kick. What I am longing to do is make that expedition into French Guinea where they got like bisexual Indians, and much of the area is unexplored. Would you be interested in such a project? Of course I need money. I will write some articles when I get myself organized. I would, of course, go to S.A. alone, but prefer someone with me. My best to Neal.

Love,
Bill

54.
August 1, 1955
Tanger

Dear Allen,

I have been ailing constantly. Neuralgia, gripe. This has interfered with my attempts to kick, but I am ready now to turn on all my reserve orgones and get the job done.

The trip to West Africa fell through, these characters being an incompetent crew of idiots and no one in his right mind would finance such an ill-conceived enterprise. I figure maybe I will take a trip through the French Zone. I simply *must* see some of this bloodshed, and nothing ever happens here.

(Just had a riot here. Details not yet available. I hear 4 casualties, all Arab, of course. All I saw was people running, shop shutters slamming down, women jerking their babies inside. So I went home and loaded my shotgun, but the riot was promptly quelled.)

As I have written, I want to make the S.A. expedition and will do so as soon as I get the $. Of course, I want to see Morocco and this whole area while I am here. I am not so interested in Europe. I feel that my real interest lies in S.A. and Mexico. If I ever got to the Far East would bog down in junk and never get out again. We only have so much time. Would you be interested in the S.A. expedition? It will be a really strenuous and dangerous trip. I want someone to go with me, but will go alone if

I have to. Figure I will need about $1000 over and above transportation.

About your poem on Joan. I think it is completely successful. I experienced a distinct shock at the end, I could see the picture of her talking and smiling so clear and precise like a telepathic image. I *knew* that I was seeing exactly what you saw. In a way a poem is a means of evoking, conveying telepathic image from the poet's mind to the mind of the reader. Baudelaire remarked on this when he spoke of poetry as a form of ritual or incantation, magic words to evoke an image or series of images in the reader's psyche. (One of the French experimenters with telepathy—I forget name, oh yes, Warcollier—excellent book, precise, clear, logical—remarks that all attempts to contact the dead telepathically resulted in images of dead-end or insuperable barriers.).

Glad to hear that Kingland visited you. Received pictures of Peter. Very attractive and nice looking. Yes you should stop nagging him for sex. It would be a basically important experience for you to visit a place like Tanger where you can have all the beautiful boys you want. I mean it enables one to separate sex, and achieve a degree of serenity.

I have only seen Bowles a few times at parties. He is very withdrawn and difficult to contact. I have done no writing lately, preoccupied with kicking and illness.

Amusing about Gregory.

Love,
Bill

Kicking is the most, in fact the *only*, important thing in my life now. *I must do it.* If I fail I will go East where I can get junk, live with it and for it from here on out. It has come to that. A definite choice for all time. I will no more be victimized by high prices, cut stuff as in U.S. I will not be harried by the law. I will not have my system wrecked by synthetics. If I use at all I want the best. I want to smoke O or use good pure M or H, and do so in ambience of calm and for a reasonable price. I give myself this summer. I either have kicked by the fall or I head East on one-way ticket.

I come near to a drug psychosis on that fucking demerol, which is the worst. I was a shaking, twitching, hallucinating wreck. I could feel my grasp of reality beginning to slip and still "one more box . . . just one more day." My body suddenly developed allergy to demerol—I puke, and headaches—literally *can't* touch it thank God!

I have supply of codeineetas to kick with, 30 tubes.

About poem on Joan Burroughs: See "Dream Record: June 8, 1955," pp. 48–49, *Reality Sandwiches* (City Lights, S.F., 1963).

55.
August 10, 1955
Tanger

Dear Allen

Ominous occurrences here. For some time past I have become acquainted, much against my will, with a local "eccentric." This citizen, an Arab, first approached me when I was strolling on the boulevard, hailed me as "his dear friend" and asked me for $50. I replied, with some asperity, that I was not his dear friend, that I had never seen him before in my life, and would not give him peseta one. Since then I run into him from time to time. His communications are progressively more cryptic: obviously he has built up an elaborate delusional system in which the U.S. Embassy is the root of all evil. I am an agent, a creature of the Embassy. I decide he is insane, probably dangerous (an uninhibited paranoid is always a bad deal). I cut the interviews as short as possible, holding myself always on the alert, ready to kick him in the stomach, arm myself with a bottle or a chair at the first hostile move. But he makes no hostile moves in my direction. In fact there is something curiously sweet about him, a strange, sinister jocularity, as if we knew each other from somewhere, and his words referred to private jokes from this period of intimacy.

On Monday, August 1, he ran amok with a razor-sharp butcher knife in the main drag, killed 5 people and wounded four, was finally cornered by the police, shot in the stomach and captured. He will recover and, unless he can prove insanity, will be shot—the form of execution obtaining here, but very rarely invoked. I wonder if he would have attacked me? I missed him by 10 minutes. The whole town is still hysterical. They shut the shops and rush inside barricading the door if anyone is seen running on the street.

The trip to West Africa never came off. They don't have the money yet. I have decided, in any case, not to go, as they are engaged in *the most dangerous* contraband operation—taking illegal diamonds *out of* W. Africa. It is five years to be found in possession of unregistered diamonds in this area. It is worse than dope. (They might hide the diamonds in my stateroom, or otherwise throw the bust into my lap.) In any case they are evil citizens, quite capable of throwing me over the side. They are lushed from wake up to pass out, they live and eat like dirty animals. All things considered, in the words of J. B. Myers: "Include me out."

I have not heard from Alan Ansen in 2 months, though he owes me a letter. Writing him today.

Perhaps we could arrange like I wait here until you arrive next year, we do Africa and Europe together, *then* make S.A. expedition. What do you think? I mean, of course, if we can get squared away financial. I certainly want someone with me who is with it. So many more angles are turned up travelling like that than alone. On the other hand, bad or indifferent company is an active detriment. I take on no excess baggage of boring or grating characters, not even if they put up the money. It's not worth it. Such personnel would ruin the trip, fuck up relations with the Indians, etc. Nor will I tolerate any prissy, prudish scientists. This is an anything goes deal, the realization of a wild routine. No sea anchors need apply.

I wrote you how much I was impressed by the poem on Joan's tomb. In fact the impression was so sharp as to be quite painful.

Please let me know how your plans shape up. What will you do when your compensation expires? Back to N.Y.? What became of Neal's third ball? Disappeared I hope. Which letter of mine did Neal groan when he read?

Love,
Bill

What will you do when your (unemployment) compensation expires?: A.G. was probably writing *Howl* just at that time.

56.
Sept. 21, 1955
Tanger

Dear Allen

Received your two letters. I am sorry to be remiss about answering. I have been so involved in attempts and preparations to evict the Chinaman once and for all. Have tentatively arranged to take a cure here. I am going to a clinic and stay there until I am completely cured. One month at least, probably two. In any case I need a period in which I will be isolated and without distraction, to organize my novel. I intend to give all my time to work during the period of cure.

Some nights ago I got hold of some ampules each containing 1/6 grain of dolophine and 1/100 grain of hyoscine. Now 1/100 gr. of that awful shit is already a lot, but I thought the dolophine would offset it and shot 6 ampules in the main line.

The ex-captain found me sitting stark naked in the hall on the toilet seat (which I had wrenched from its moorings), playing in a bucket of water and singing "Deep in the Heart of Texas," at the same time complaining, in clearly enunciated tones, of the high cost of living—"It all goes into razor blades." And I attempted to go out in the street naked at 2 A.M.—What a horrible nightmare if I had succeeded and came to myself wandering around the Native Quarter naked. I tore up my sheets and threw bottles all over the floor, looking for something, I did not say what. Naturally Dave and the Old Dutch Auntie who runs this whorehouse were alarmed, thinking my state was permanent. They were vastly relieved to see me the following morning fully dressed and in my right mind. I could only remember snatches of what had happened, but I do remember wondering why people were looking at me so strangely and talking in such tiresome, soothing voices. I concluded they were crazy or drunk, and told Tony he was stinking drunk.

I have read over your poem many times, and think it is one of the best things you have done. How is your book coming? I am on pretty good terms with Paul Bowles now, but still don't know him well enough to ask his opinion on a Ms.

This character who makes it with son and daughter sounds rather engaging. What are your plans for the next year? I heard from Jack in Mexico City. Dave is dead. I wrote Garver why the hell didn't he go to the Far East or to Persia where they got like *opium shops*, and get what he wants instead of subsisting on a miserable diet of codeine pills. The man has no gumption left. It is too much for him to get on a boat or a plane (almost as cheap now. You can fly from Tanger to N.Y. for $300.). Those places are too "far away" though from what I can't understand. Also they are vaguely dangerous. With his income and his one track mind, I would be on my way to Teheran or Hong Kong tomorrow. That's what I would do if I intended to stay on junk. I would go somewhere I could get the real stuff cheap and legal.

Your moment of illumination very interesting, especially the flowers.

In your place I would take a firm stand with Peter's brother and his appetite. Sounds to me like he needs a boot in the ass figuratively and literally. I mean why kowtow to an obnoxious young punk? My love to Jack if he has arrived. I hope to enter clinic in two days.

Love,
Bill

Your moment of illumination very interesting, especially the flowers: Probably a reference to "Transcription of Organ Music," pp. 25–27, *Howl* (City Lights, S.F., 1956).

Peter's brother: Lafcadio Orlovsky.

57.
[October 1955]
[Tanger]

[Beginning of letter missing]

I have a short story written in longhand which I will type and send along. Will also do an article on Yage. But most important I want to do some definite work on my novel about Interzone. If I can really concentrate on that I have a chance to kick this habit. But I never felt less creative . . .

Why do you take all this crap from Peter's brother? People are better off if they don't get all they want to eat. It's been proved with rats.

The Arabs are more and more hostile and insolent and sullen and insufferable. Just now a kid rapped on my window and asked me for a cigarette. I told him to shove off, and he continued banging on the window until I picked up a cane and started out the door. I would have hit him with the cane if I caught him. I hate these people and their cowardly, sniveling, stupid hostility. Another trick they have is putting banana peels on the door step.

Oct. 7 [1955]

I just went to see the woman in a strange Kafkian bureau built into a massive stone arch. I have passed it every day and never noticed the office was there: Office of Social Assistance it is called. Within ten minutes she had conjured up a doctor who will treat me, and procured me a room in the Jewish Hospital. Private room where I can use my typewriter, for $2 per day! I am going to stay there until I am cured. At least a month, more likely two. Checking in tomorrow morning. I can hardly believe it. Hope there is no last minute slip-up. My introduction to this woman came about through an old English mooch and drunk. For the past five months I have been giving him a little money several times a week. Everybody told me it was a waste of money but I persisted. Like a fairy story, what?

The dollar is going up like a beautiful bird.

Strange, vivid junk-sick dreams lately, permeated with a feeling of nostalgia and loss. Well, now I have two months to do nothing but write. I will see what I can accomplish. One reason I want to make the S.A.

expedition is it will give me something definite to write about. Any news of Jack? Please write to me.

Love,
Bill

P.S. Finally bought a typewriter. Brand new for $46. A real bargain.

No telling what I will do after my cure. Figure to make up for lost time, and I never want to see any more junk.

The Yage article might sell. I have those photos to go with it you know.

And maybe in two months I'll have something to show a publisher on the novel. We will see.

Maybe I will go East overland, right on around the world and come to see you from the East.

Once I get off Junk anything is possible.

You really should dig South America. More interesting than Africa or Europe. I will dig up the money someway. I might even write something that will sell. The prospect of cure has given me a concentration of energy I haven't had for months.

The English mooch who got me in touch with this woman is blossoming out in new clothes and all manner of schemes to make a fortune. Who knows but what I may get in on something good? I am already paid back for the money I gave him and the meals and drinks I bought, by this introduction. I had tried two doctors, every hospital and clinic in town, and finally gave up. It seemed like no hospital or clinic would accept a case of addiction. Then Leslie told me to go see this woman and gave me a note to her. Tanger has more people stranded without money than any place I ever saw, but no one had ever heard of this woman, who doles out all manner of assistance to any inhabitant of Tanger regardless of nationality. I could have got the treatment free most likely but I didn't want any delay. Besides the price is so low.

Well Love again and Good Bye for now.

Write to Legation, Kiki will pick up my mail there and bring it to me.

Bill

58.
*Letter B
(written before I got your letter)
Benchimal Hosp.
Tanger
Oct. 21, 1955*

Dear Allen,

Letter A is the beginning of chapter II of Interzone novel. Chapter II is almost complete. About 40 pages. I will send along in next week or so.

Still getting 40 Mg shot of dolophine every 4 hours (That = about 1 grain of M.). Only halfway comfortable cure I ever took. It will take about two months. When I leave here I will be completely off, able to drink and function *sans* junk.

Chapter II is: *Selections from Lee's Letters and Journals.* With this gimmick I can use all letters including love letters, fragmentary material, anything. Of course I am not using anywhere near all the letters. I will often sort through 100 pages to concoct 1 page. Funny though how the letters hang together. I figure to use one sentence and it pulls a whole page along with it. The selection is difficult, and, of course, tentative—(I have letters from past year, and long hand notes of past six months)—This is a first draft, a sort of frame work. I plan to alternate chapters of Letter and Journal Selections, with straight narrative chapters like Chapter I. May end up relegating the Letter and Journal chapters to an appendix. We will see. In next two months I should have enough completed to show a publisher if there is a publisher who will look at it. The selection chapters form a sort of mosaic with the cryptic significance of juxtaposition like objects abandoned in a hotel drawer, a form of still life.

Reading over my letters I have thought a lot about you. By all means you should come here as soon as possible. But it is much better deal you come here than I should go to Frisco. The U.S. is no place for me. I need a place with more room, more leeway.

My mind is turning to crime lately. "Strange things I have in heart that will to hand." Of all crimes blackmail must be the most artistically satisfying, I mean The Moment of Truth when you see his front, his will to resist, collapse. That must be real tasty. I mention this angle in Chapter II.

This writing is more painful than anything I ever did. Parentheses pounce on me and tear me apart. I have no control over what I write, which is as it should be. I feel like the St. Anthony of Hieronymus Bosch or however his name goes.

I have book of Klee's work and writing. Terrific. The pictures are literally alive. Have Genet's *Journal of a Thief* in English, and have read it over many times. I think he is one of the greatest living writers of prose. Dig this: He is being fucked by a big Negro in the Santé Prison: "I shall be crushed by his darkness which will gradually dilute me. With my mouth open, I shall know he is in a torpor, held in that dark axis by his steel pivot. I shall gaze over the world with that clear gaze the eagle loaned to Ganymede." The translation is not bad except for the dialogue. He translates into outmoded U.S. slang. I mean nobody now talks like this: "I'll drill somebody for just a little loose cash." Terrible. Why not leave the French argot and explain meaning?

Reading over your poems and letters: The following lines strike me from *Siesta in Xbalba*: "That register indifferent greeting across time." . . . "Vanished out of the fading grip of stone hands." . . . the whole stanza beginning: "Time's slow wall o'ertopping etc." is superb . . . "Like burning, screaming lawyers" HMMMM . . . One line shockingly bad: "And had I money" . . . The poem as a whole very good, but cannot compare, *as a unified piece of work*, with your *Strophes*, which is really all in one piece and to my mind the best thing you have done. I do not single out lines, because it is all excellent. I believe I already wrote you that the poem on Joan's grave gave me a very distinct shock—because of personal associations—almost unpleasantly intense. The poem is certainly a success.

Your mystic moment with "the glistening animal aspect of the flowers" reminds me of Yage intoxication. So does the work of Klee. One of his pictures entitled "Indiscretion" is exact copy of what I saw high on Yage in Pucallpa when I closed my eyes.

A good selection of people in Tanger now: Dave Lamont, young Canadian painter who comes to see me every day; Chris Wanklyn, Canadian writer; Paul and Jane Bowles quite accessible these days; Charles Gallager, extremely intelligent and witty, writing history of Morocco on Ford Foundation; Viscount des Iles, a brilliant linguist and student of the occult; Peter Mayne, who wrote *The Alleys of Marrakesh*. In short, plenty people around now. I hope you can make it here real soon. Love to Neal and Jack if he is there,

Love,
Bill

P.S. Like very much *At Sunset* and *Her Engagement*. The Wallace Stevens poem is real great. The best thing he has done. I never liked him before.

Your *Strophes*: Probably early Ms. of *Howl*.
The Wallace Stevens poem is real great: Probably "Lebensweisheitspeilerei" ending with "In the stale grandeur of annihilation." "At Sunset" and "Her Engagement", probably poems by A.G., are now forgotten.

59.
Letter C
Benchimal Hosp.
Tanger
Oct. 23, 1955

Dear Allen and Jack,

Kiki just brought me your letter—no date on it—I don't want to give you the impression I'm like on my way to Frisco, because it ain't necessarily so like a lot of things you're liable to read in my letters. To begin with I got no loot. I wrote you from the withdrawal doldrums. Actually Tanger is looking up—What I mean to say is I don't know what the fuck I will do when I get out of here and that is a pact/I mean a fact. There's a war here I want to dig, also *Perganum Harmala* which is same thing as Yage used by Berbers, also *Barrio Chino* of Barcelona that Genet writes about and the rest of Spain for which I feel an affinity; may make overland trip to Persia with Charles Gallagher, may visit Ansen in Venice, would like to dig Yugoslavia and the queer monasteries of Greece. Also figure to start at one end of Interzone and screw my way through to the other. I am tired of monogamy with Kiki . . . Dryden speaks of the Golden Age: "Ere one to one was cursedly confined." Let's get on back to that Golden Age . . . Like the song say, "A boy's will is the wind's will." Besides which my mind is seething with ideas to make a $ (some of them not exactly legit). The

Nice Night Nurse just give me a bang and it is hitting me right in the gut, a soft, sweet blow . . . I call her "The Nice Night Nurse" to distinguish her from the bitch who gave me a shot of plain water a few nights back, I suspect her to be a schmecker but it's hard to tell with women and Chinamen. Anyhoo I don't want her ministering to me no more. (Just went to the head again. Still locked. Locked for six solid hours. I think they are using it as an operating room.) I am getting sexy, come three times last night. The Italian school is just opposite, and I stand for hours watching the boys with my 8-power field glasses. Curious feeling of projecting myself, like I was standing over there with the boys, invisible earthbound ghost, torn with disembodied lust. They wear shorts, and I can see the goose pimples on their legs in the chill of the morning, count the hairs—Did I ever tell you about the time Marv and I paid two Arab kids sixty cents to watch them screw each other—we demanded semen too, no half assed screwing— So I asked Marv: "Do you think they will do it?" and he says: "I think so. They are hungry." They did it. Made me feel sorta like a dirty old man . . . Frisco sounds like kicks and I would love to dig all of you, I mean you, Allen, and Jack, you, and sweet Neal . . . Your letter thawed out my bleak, windswept psyche— At times lately I come on downright mean. Jump all over the Arab servants. I am the most unpopular patient in this malodorous trap. Talk about hospital smell . . . you ain't had it till you sniff a Spanish Hospital. You all shame me with your Buddhistic love and sweetness, torn as I am by winds of violence and discord . . . Glad to hear that you are getting some $ on your work. No one deserves it more. What is the HOWL Allen read? The reading sounds really great. Wish I could have been there. So I should bring Kiki with me? I'll find plenty young boys around there? Come now, Allen what's this you're hinting at? Who are these important people who are mad at me? Dirty VIP's. It's about time you wised up to Trilling. He's a type can't and won't do you any good anyway. He's got no orgones, no *mana*, no charge to him. Just soaks up your charge to keep the battery of his brain turning out crap for the *Partisan Review*. Publishing in those obituary pages is really the kiss of death, the very fuck of death. That pornography reads real nice, I'd like to see it all. Now look, sweetheart, you are my agent so see what you can do with this Interzone deal. You will have about a hundred pages in next two months . . . Twenty percent . . . But I have wandered off the point, out of contact, fallen into a great gray gap between parentheses. Sit back and look blankly at the letter . . . No I can't neither be no fucking monk. Really I am dubious of the land of the free, not overkeen to walkabout long Stateside in those great boyless spaces . . . but *quien sabe*? I may decide on Frisco. Of course, if I latched onto some gelt, I would sure come to visit *en route* to South America . . . Your letter has a warming, heartening, relaxing effect on me. Yes I would like to see old Garver again before he dies. Tell Neal from me to drop the bang tails. You can't beat it. Dream hunches are *not supposed to be used that way*. You understand, Neal? You know what horse is going to win, but you *cannot use that knowledge to make money*. Don't try. It's like fighting a ghost antagonist who can hit you but you can't hit him. Drop it. Forget it. Keep your money . . .

I am progressing towards complete lack of caution and restraint. Nothing must be allowed to dilute my routines. I know I used to be shy about approaching boys, for example, but I cannot remember why exactly. The centers of inhibition are atrophied, occluded like an eel's ass on The Way to Sargasso—good book title. You know about eels? When they reach full maturity, they leave the streams and ponds of Europe traveling downstream to the sea, they cross the Atlantic Ocean to the Sargasso Sea—near Bermuda—where they mate and die. During this perilous journey they stop eating and their ass holes seal over. The young eels start back for the fresh water ponds and streams of Europe— Say that's better than *Ignorant Armies* (Dover Beach by Arnold) as a title for my Interzone novel:

Meet Me in Sargasso, I'll See You in Sargasso, The Sargasso Trail

Death opens the door of his old green pickup and says to The Hitchhiker: "You look occluded, friend. Going straight through to Sargasso?"

Ticket for Sargasso, Meet in Sargasso, On the Road to Sargasso—what I want to convey, though, is the *inner* pull towards Sargasso: *Sargasso Yen, Sargasso Time, Sargasso Kicks, The Sargasso Blues,* I can't get it. This is all trivial, doesn't convey those eels wiggling across fields at night in the wet grass to find the next pond or stream, thousands dying on the way . . . If I ever buy a boat, I will call it *The Sargasso* . . . *Sargasso Junction, Change for Sargasso, Sargasso Transfer, Sargasso Detour*—*basta* . . . Do you know about lampreys? When they mate they tear each other with their suction cups so that they always die afterwards. Either a prey to other fish—or to virginal lampreys—or infiltrated by fungus.

Some of this letter I am transcribing into Letter A which is the beginning of chapter II. Material often overlaps. You are free to choose, add, subtract, rearrange if you find a potential publisher. This is Sat., and the letter can't go off before Monday. I will be adding to it. May come up with *the* Sargasso title. So thanks for your letter and good bye for now . . . See you in Sargasso . . . One of the Sargasso titles might do for my story about Tiger Ted . . .

Love,
Bill

Yesterday I took a walk on the outskirts of town. Environs of the Zone are wildly beautiful. Low hills with great variety of trees, flowering vines and shrubs, great, red sandstone cliffs topped with curiously stylized,

Japanese-looking pine trees, fall to the sea. What a place for a house on top of those cliffs!

I used to complain I lacked material to write about. Mother of God! Now I'm swamped with material. I could write 50 pages on that walk, which was a mystical vision comparable to your East Harlem Revelations— That letter where I come on sorta whiny like: "Tanger has nothing for me and it's all your fault I'm here anyhoo."

Well, Al, 'tain't necessarily so. Beginning to dig Arab kicks. It takes time. You must let them seep into you . . . Weel like I say I could write a book on that walk. Instead I will select one moment:

I went in an Arab café for a glass of mint tea. One room 15 by 15, a few tables and chairs, a raised platform covered with mats stretched across one end of the room where the Arabs sit with their shoes off playing cards and smoking kif, the inevitable picture of Ben Yussef, The Deposed Sultan—you see his undistinguished pan everywhere like those pictures of my fran Roosevelt—pictures of Mecca done in the hideous light pinks and blues of religious objects, profoundly vulgar like the final, decadent phase of Aztec mosaics—Pawing through this appalling mass of notes and letters, looking for something, I run across one of your old letters, Al, and the following jumps out at me: "Don't be depressed. There's too much to do." And that *is* a fact. So much I am flipping. You're a fucking genius, Al . . .

I draw some dirty looks from a table of Arabs and stare at them till they drop their eyes and fumble with kif pipes. If they insist to make something out of it, I'd as soon die now as anytime. It is as Allah wills. Here on the red tile floor of this café, with a knife in my kidney, you dig one of them slipped around me. I always carry a knife myself, and I would get the best price I could in the blood and flesh of my opponents. I'm not one to turn the other kidney. The metaphysics of interpersonal combat: Zen Buddhist straightaheadedness applied to fencing and knife fighting, Jiu-Jitsu principle of "winning by giving in" and

"Turning your opponent's strength against him," various techniques of knife fighting, a knife fight as a mystic contest, a discipline like Yoga—You must eliminate fear and anger—and see the fight as a impersonal process. Like primitive drawing depicts parts of an animal the artist can not see—spinal column, heart, stomach—though he know they are there—see *Arts of the South Seas* by Ralph Linton—so the knife fighter sees the inner organs of his opponent; heart, liver, stomach, neck veins, that he is attempting to externalize and delineate with his knife. Or you can conceive it as cool and cerebral as chess, a game involving the barter of pain and blood in which you try to get for your boy, your golden body, the best deal possible. Jiu-Jitsu proverb: You give your muscles— Let him knock you around—You take his bones . . . In knife fight you must be ready to give without hesitating your left arm and your face. You take a liver, a stomach, a carotid artery . . .

Not that I even look for or want any kind of a fight, and a man has to be out of line to seek a fight with me— It almost never happens— The knife fight potential was simply one facet of that moment, sitting in the café, looking out at the hill opposite, stylized pine trees on top arranged with the economy of a Chinese print against blue sky in the tingling, clear, classic Mediterranean air . . . I was completely alive in the moment, not saving myself, not waiting for anything or anybody—"I have told no one to wait"—This is it right now . . . Some French writer said: "Only those who love life do not fear death." So don't ever worry about your boy Willy Lee, Al. I quote from one of your letters: "You lose sight of life, lose vigor, become dependent and listless, become a drag, sink, lose blood, junk up, crawl off threatening to die." Sounds like advertisement describing the victim of a sluggish colon . . ."And then I took Ma Lee's Orgone Yeast! WOW!"

Actually I am so independent, so fucking far out I am subject to float away like a balloon . . .

Today's walk was different. More incident, less revelation. Actual fight in another café. Minor fracas. Hitting each other with their heavy, rubber-soled sandals. No knives, no broken glasses, no blood . . . Nothing tasty. The proprietor, a young kid, left when the fight started . . . The fight just suddenly stopped for no reason . . . Well that's Africa, son . . . The proprietor came back with another kid, walking with arms around each other's ribs, and gave me a dazzling smile when I got up to pay for my tea . . . On the walk I was thinking: "All complete swish fairies should be killed, not as traitors to the cause of queerness, but for selling out the human race to the forces of negation and death. Kill the nanny beater too. "Let petty kings the names of parties know; where 'er I come I kill both friend and foe." How do you know when a man is "complete fairy?" *"De carne tumefacta y pensamiento in mundo Maricas de los ciudades . . . Madres de lode, enmigos sin sueño del Amor, Que dais a los muchachos gotas de suicia muerte con amargo veneno."* Garcia Lorca, "Ode to Walt Whitman." Translates: "You fucking fairies of the cites—" he has just said he don't object to queers as such— "With rotten flesh and filthy thoughts. Mother of mud, sleepless enemies of love, who give to boys drops of dirty death with bitter venom" Hear! Hear! . . . They *never* would be missed. And how do you know anybody is in that class? *They* know . . . They are self-condemned. You can see it in their eyes. A judge in Interzone who will listen to no evidence, doesn't want to know what a man is accused of . . . He just looks into his eyes and acquits or passes sentence . . . Complete lack of quantitative orientation leads to a sort of divine madness . . . So be it.

Saw an Arab boy incredibly delicate and fragile, wrists like thin brown sticks.

Well I gotta get back to Interzone novel. Imshay Allah—God willing—I complete chapter II today and start on narrative chapters. I tell you sifting through those letters and notes for usable material is a labor of Hercules.

Two weeks I am hung up on this selection chapter. Everytime I try to terminate it, another routine pounces on me. I will keep a sort of diary of my cure. I mean the above is my page for today . . . Maybe I should be a columnist yet. Sell me to a newspaper, Al. You're my agent.

What is the *Howl* Allen read? The reading sounds really great: Reference to "6 Poets at 6 Gallery" reading Sept. or Oct. 1955 S.F.—Rexroth, the interlocutor, younger poets Lamantia, McClure, Whalen, Ginsberg, and Snyder vocalizing their work for the first time.

60.
Nov. 1, 1955
[Tanger]

Dear Jack & Al,

Arab Café: Sat down and had three words . . . just three long words, with Miss Green. Really I never knew That One to come on so wild anyplace else, I mean not with such wild kicks . . . I've known her to get more *physical* other places, but that was in another country and besides . . . Watching a glass of mint tea on a bamboo mat in the sun, the steam blow back into the glass top like smoke from a chimney . . . It seemed to have some special significance like an object spotted in a movie . . . I was thinking like a book you read which also has pictures and accompanying music.

Some Arabs at a table. I am sitting there watching the cup of tea. It is unthinkable they should molest me . . . Suppose they do? And suddenly they have seized me, and are preparing to castrate me? It can't happen . . . must be a dream . . . In Interzone it might or might not be a dream, and which way it falls might be in the balance while I watch this tea glass in the sun . . . The meaning of Interzone, its space time location is at a point where three-dimensional fact merges into dream, and dreams erupt into the real world . . . In Interzone dreams can kill—Like Bangutot—and solid objects and persons can be unreal as dreams . . . For example Lee could be in Interzone, after killing the two detectives, and for various dream reasons, neither the law nor The Others could touch him directly . . . Similarly, it looks easy to assassinate the Spanish Politico, but as The Boy told Lee: "It's not as easy as it looks. He's well protected . . ."

"You mean secret police . . . "

"Oh there will be secret police, of course . . . No I didn't imply you were stupid enough to need worry about *them* . . . What I mean is a very different kind of protection."

All letters off today. Will probably be sending along something every 5 days or so.

Love,
Bill

Bangutot: S.E. Asian nightmare-death-strangulation sickness. See p. 71, *Naked Lunch* (Evergreen paperback, N.Y., 1966).

61.
Nov. 2, 1955
[Tanger]

Dear Jack and Allen,

Tanger is the prognostic pulse of the world, like a dream extending from past into the future, a frontier between dream and reality—the "reality" of both called into question . . .

No one here is what they seem on the surface. Take my last doctor, from Strasbourg. The best physician in Tanger; seems at first sight a typical European intellectual. (He asked me if I thought schedule feeding had any bearing on drug addiction . . . real sharp you dig—), passes himself off as Anti-Nazi, Jewish refugee, says he is a doctor first, not a businessman . . . Radiates high-class Jewish honesty . . . The first hint I get that all is not kosher with him is in that other clinic where he come near killing me with his fucking cold turkey sleep cure . . . I gave him $4 and wrote out a telegram to send my parents asking for more money . . . Next day I asked if he sent the telegram and he said yes but did not bother to give me a receipt, that is he didn't bother for the good reason that there was no receipt. He never sent the telegram. He kept the money. It seemed so out of character I put it out of my mind, almost believing I had made a mistake . . . Then I began to notice other little things . . . Like his bill was out of line by about $30. . . I paid what I thought reasonable, and he never said any more about it . . . In short he had simply given me a large bill hoping I would pay it and say nothing. Instead I said nothing and didn't pay it. I paid half . . . "God!" It hit me suddenly leaving his office. "An Arab trick! Ask outrageous price and settle for half!" Later I found out he was no Anti-Nazi refugee, but a collaborator who got out of Strasbourg just ahead of the French 'Partisans . . . Withal he is still the best physician in Tanger . . .

"Oh *Him*" the gossip chorus says . . . "Notorious collaborator, my dear, *and* he's, well, *queer* for money."

So what does he do with the money . . . Addict? Uh-uh, not with that careful, anal face, without a trace of oral impulsiveness. No junky, no lush he. Boys? No, the queens would have smelled him out, bitched him out years ago . . . But not the maddest gossips in Tanger ever said he was queer. Women? Uh-uh . . . he looks like he "gets that over with" about once every two weeks . . . Besides the chorus of Old Women in The Port Tea Room cover that entrance . . .

There are two potentials. No 1: He is a modern miser—He's not the type to fill a bathtub with gold coins and roll around on them naked—No, I mean a Security Miser who keeps his family on starvation rations (funny you can tell by looking at him he has no appreciation for food, would set a tasteless table)—

[Remainder of letter missing.]

62.
Dec. 10, 1955
Tanger

Dear Allen,

I forgot to include description of the boys screwing (it always annoys me when someone ignores a question in one of my letters). I will call them Boy 1. and Boy 2. Boy 1. is a beautiful kid, thin, small, with delicate features of S.E. Asiatic cast. Looks like one type Mexican Indian. Copper-coloured skin, fine straight black hair. Boy 2. is beautiful but has a stupid, peasant look to him—he is in fact from the Hills. His features are not sharply distinguished. He could be American, German, anything.

We took the two boys back to Dave's room and told them what we wanted. After some coy giggling they agreed, and took off their ragged clothes. Both of them had slender, beautiful boy bodies. Dave was M.C. He pointed to Boy 2. and said: "All right you screw him first" pointing to Boy 1. Boy 1. lay down on his stomach on the bed. Boy 2. rubbed spit on his prick and began screwing him . . . Dave said: "*Leche* we want *leche.*" *Leche* means milk. Spanish for jissum—(The boy contracted convulsively and his breath whistled through his teeth. He lay still for a moment on top of the other boy then shoved himself off with both hands. He showed us the jissum on his prick and asked for a towel. Dave threw him one and he carefully wiped his prick. Then he lay down on his stomach and Boy 1. took over. He was more passionate. He got mad because Boy 2. kept his ass contracted and pounded on his buttocks with his fist. Finally he got it in and began screwing violently. Boy 2. groaned in protest. Boy 1. came almost immediately, his buttocks quivered in spasms. He sighed and then rolled free . . . I see both boys every day. They will do it anytime for forty cents which is standard price.

As to why "And had I money" is bad. No it isn't the inversion. It's the jarring banality. Like I should insert a recipe for curry in the middle of the Yage City vision. The whole concept is flat, unpoetic. It doesn't belong and should be removed at once. It mars the whole stanza, in fact the whole poem—since a poem is, or should be, all one piece, and suffers more than prose from a really bad passage. And believe me, "And had I money" is really bad.

Dozed off and seemed to have been for years in some prison camp where I suffered from malnutrition . . . It could refer to junk, of course, but that wouldn't explain the malnutrition which seemed to be the point. I often fall asleep while writing and see problems that occupy me in symbolic visual form. At night I take sleeping pills, then work until I feel sleepy. These are a new type pill. You don't feel sleepy. You just suddenly fall asleep. I have fallen asleep reading in a chair and slept for four hours. The pills have no after-effect—did you ever have a goofball hangover? Terrible. Depression and a horrible barbiturate feeling in the stomach. Like all metabolic states, the real essence of it can not be conveyed verbally, I mean the quality by which I recognize it at once as a barbiturate hangover.

Went to bed with Kiki this afternoon. He is very quick and intuitive. I told him, after I had come and we were laying around smoking, that a friend of mine might be coming here soon from America. He said right away: "Allen?" Now I never said anything to him about you except he saw your picture and asked who you were and I said you were my best friend.

[Remainder of letter missing.]

63.
Feb. 17, 1956
Tanger

Dear Allen,

The way things break lately it's like there was a vast Kafkian conspiracy to prevent me from ever getting off junk. At the beginning of the month I almost had money to get to England. I wrote for more, asking them to cable it. Ten days later they cable me $100, but by then I am almost $100 in debt to the ex-captain who lives next door (not only dishonest but impractical to leave without paying him). So I telegraph I need $100 more. That was a week ago, and no answer to my telegram. Meanwhile the $100 is half gone, there isn't another boat until the 20th, and by then this $100 is all gone, and even another $100 isn't enough to get me to England. I mean the way they feed me $ a little bit at a time, I never have enough to move. And then they say "Money is so short now we want to be sure it isn't wasted" while doling it out in such a way I have no alternative but to waste it.

The shipment of dolophine arrived finally, but now is running low again. Not only do I have a habit, but a synthetic habit which is hardest to kick, most harmful to the health, and the least enjoyable. And I am never sure from one day to the next of my supply—though it is never cut off long enough for me to switch to codeine. All in all I have fallen into a state of chronic depression and hopelessness. All I can do is sit here day after day shivering and contracted over my stinking little kerosene stove waiting for money.

Trouble in Tanger lately. A friend of mine waylaid and stabbed in the back for no reason, not ever robbery. (In the lung. He will be all right.) The old Dutch pimp who runs the place where I used to live set upon by five Arabs and beaten to a pulp. An Argentinian queer severely beaten by a gang of youths. I will try to pick up a pistol some place. It's really getting to a point where you need one.

I am typing up one version of the Yage article in what I hope will be acceptable form. I will send this on to you together with the Tanger article which is completed and typed.

Terrible weather here. Cold and wet and windy.

Love,
Bill

64.
Sun. Feb. 26, 1956
Tanger

Dear Allen,

Still in a condition of biostasis, waiting on money to reach England. I will definitely get away when my $200 comes next week.

I just experienced indescribable nightmare flash of my physical helplessness: wherever I go and whatever I do I am always in the strait-jacket of junk, unable to move a finger to free myself, like I was paralyzed by an anaesthetic, and suddenly realized that my will had no power to move my body. I keep dozing off into dreams or structural presentations of thought.

President Eisenhower is a junkie, but can't take it directly because of his position, so he gets his junk kicks through me. He doesn't have to be with me, but from time to time we have to make contact, and I recharge him. These contacts look, to the casual observer, like homosexual practices, but looking closer one observes that the excitement is not sexual, and the climax is the separation when the recharge is completed, not union or any counterfeit or symbol of union. The erect penises are brought in contact—at least we used that method in the beginning, but contact points wear out just like veins. Now I sometimes have to slip my penis under his left eyelid. Of course I can always give him an osmosis recharge—which corresponds to a skin shot—but that is admitting defeat. An O.R.—Osmosis Recharge—will put the President in a bad mood for weeks and might well result in Atomic Shambles. For the President pays a high price for the Oblique Habit. A whole spectrum of subjective horror, silent protoplasmic agonies, bone frenzies, is known only to the man with an Oblique Habit. Tensions build up, pure energy without emotional content finally tears through the body, throwing him about like a man in contact with high-tension wires. Sometimes, if his charge connection is cut off cold, the Oblique Addict falls into such violent electric convulsions that his bones shake loose and he dies with the skeleton straining to climb out of his unendurable flesh. The Oblique Addict has sacrificed all control. He is helpless as a child in the womb.

The relation between an O.A. (Oblique Addict) and his R.C.(Recharge Connection—often jokingly referred to as his RX) is so intense that they can only endure each other's company for brief infrequent intervals (I mean aside from the R.M.—Recharge Meets—when all personal contact is eclipsed by the recharge process).

Conversation piece. Two elegant pansies in excruciatingly chic apartment.

P. 1: (Bursting into the room) "My dear, you'll never guess what I've got . . . Lab reports just in . . . Leprosy!"

P. 2: How *Medieval* of you!

P. 1: I'm having a black cloak designed by Antoine. Absolutely authentic. And I shall carry a bell . . .

P. 2: Oh they'll most likely arrest you before anything really picturesque develops . . . Everything is curable these days. If only we could have a real old corny plague . . . You know, corpses sprawled sexily about the street . . . those *boy* corpses, dungarees tight over the basket, lying there so helpless, so *young* . . . For Gawd's sake Myrtle bring a basin for me to drool in . . . And mixed with the smell of decay and death there was another smell seeping through the bolted doors, the shuttered windows: the sharp, acrid smell of fear . . . I suppose I'm a hopeless romantic . . ."

P. 1: One thing I do ask of you, of all my dear friends—God rot the silly bitches—leave us have no mealy-mouthed blather about "Hansen's Disease—"

Character for novel: rich, queer leper who is not supposed to frequent Turkish Baths or swimming pools. They keep a plainclothes man on him at all times, and he is always trying to shake his shadow so he can get to a Turkish bath for "a spot of good unclean fun." I think he's English but not sure yet. Can't see him good on account of the steam.

"You've no idea the money I save" he says. "When I show the little beasts my card—all God's lepers got cards with their fingerprints, photograph, and number. I managed to wangle number 69. It took some doing—they generally bolt without even thinking about *fluss*."

This letter is the only writing I have done in a week now. In the grey limbo of junk I seem to depend on you as my only point of reference. Well, Imshah-Allah (with Allah's endorsement) I will be out of this sneak preview of Hell by this time next week. Telegram from home that

$200 is on the way. As soon as I get my hands on it, I take the next plane out of here.

Tanger Monday—Feb. 27, 1956: I expect my getaway money this week. Probably this afternoon or tomorrow. Then the plane for London—there is a plane every morning that gets in London about 2 o'clock of the same afternoon. So hold up any communications until I write you from England. I haven't heard from you in some weeks, and hope you are at the same address and receiving my letters. You spoke of a trip to Seattle, but I presumed, since you said nothing to the contrary, that you were keeping the place at Milvia Street and would return there, or had arranged to have mail forwarded. Before I leave here I will send you the Tanger article, and one version of the Yage article which I am typing up as neatly and accurately as I can.

If I don't make it in England, I am coming back Stateside and give myself up in Lexington. I simply will not travel with this Chinaman any longer. Taking so much I keep going on the nod. Last night I woke up with someone squeezing my hand. It was my own other hand. Or I fall half asleep reading something and the words change or take on a curious dream significance as if I was reading code. Obsessed with codes lately. Like a man contracts a series of illnesses which spell out a message. Or he gets message from subsidiary personality by farting in Morse code. (Naturally to say such obvious devices as automatic writing would never get by the Censor.)

I believe I wrote you the natives are getting uppity. Time for some counter-terrorism, seems to me. The police are quite worthless, the Arab police now quite openly taking sides against Europeans or Americans in any *contretemps*. A number of queers got notes warning them to leave town and signed "The Red Hand". (No note for me.) As usual, Puritanism and Nationalism come on together in a most disagreeable *mélange*.

Degenerate spectacle: I just hit a vein (not easy these

days. I don't got many veins left). So I kissed the vein, calling it "my sweet little needle sucker," and talked baby talk to it.

Did you read about the five missionaries killed by the Auca Indians in Ecuador? I'd like to try contacting the Auca. Nobody has succeeded in making contact with them. Might drop kegs of paregoric from a plane until they all got a habit. See myself surrounded by sick Auca: "You make medicine heap quick!" They found some films on the dead missionaries. You see they contacted one group of Auca and thought they were in. Their last radio message was: "A group of Auca we haven't seen before has just arrived." The pictures show them as a fine-looking people, completely naked. As for the missionaries, it's no loss. I've met them in S.A. and they are a perfect plague. Telling the Indians they shouldn't chew cocaine or take Yage or drink their homemade liquor, they should put on clothes. I mean all the old missionary crap. And such stupid, ignorant, ugly-looking people. I hate them. And they teach the Indians to sing their ugly, Protestant hymns. The father of one of the dead missionaries (they were all killed with spears, by the way, except one who was killed with one of the machetes they had given to the Indians) remarked rather enigmatically on learning of his son's death: "God doesn't make any mistakes."

That picture you sent of the cops in women's clothes, I had already seen in the local Spanish paper here. It has quite good news coverage, but like all Spanish papers, completely controlled by the Franco government, the virtues of which they are continually editorializing. Enclose a picture I drew. I started doodling, with no idea as to what I intended to draw, and it just took shape and seems to have a sort of life. I call it "The Blind Mouth." (When I was a child I thought you saw with your mouth. I remember distinctly my brother telling me no, with the eyes, and I closed my eyes and found out it was true and my theory was wrong.)

I still haven't written to Jack. Must do so.

Gag for Milton Berle: Feller say I reckon Christ got Mary's immaculate cherry on the way out.

Love,
Bill

[*Fluss:* Arab word meaning "money."]

You spoke of a trip to Seattle: Taken with Gary Snyder, hitchhiking, a reading tour.

1624 Milvia Street: A backyard cottage in Berkeley described by Kerouac in *Desolation Angels* and *Dharma Bums*. A.G. had lived there with Whalen, Snyder, and Kerouac at various times, Peter and others visiting, circa 1955–56.

65.
March 14, 1956
[Tanger]

Dear Allen,

Just got your letter of Feb. 26. My father writes I should wait here until he makes arrangements with a sanitarium in England. I am inclined to go on and see if I can't arrange to get free treatment—(The thing to do nowadays is to get one's snout in the public trough). I am only deterred by the possibility of being hung up in London *sans* junk and *sans* sanitarium. I know they licence addicts in England but don't know whether that applies to foreigners. There is an English doctor here who might be able to give me the info. Right offhand it seems rather unlikely they would welcome alien junkies with open arms and immediate junk permits. But *quien sabe?* Trying to decide whether to go on now or wait, I have fallen into a sort of *folie de doute*, waiting for a sign to make up my mind. God knows I don't want my father to spend an unnecessary cent on the deal. Also I want to get away from this horrible, synthetic shit.

I had not seen any of this material before. It was not in the first copy you sent me. I don't wonder the poem is causing a stir. Like I say, it seems to me definitely the best thing you have done as a sustained whole. The "I'm With You in Rockland" section excellent and very moving. I like especially the stanza that contains "starry spangled shock of mercy".

I just fell asleep for a moment and had a flash of dream: a policeman on a bicycle, screaming with shrill lust, following a boy down a long, dusty road in Mexico. In the distance is a river with trees growing along the banks, and on the other side of the river a town.

Moloch stanzas excellent. Where do they fit in exactly? Be sure to send me copy of the whole poem as soon as you get copy. It is finished now and ready for publication by Crazy Lights?? This poem is undoutably the best thing you have done; also, it seems to me, the end of one line of development. I am wondering where you will go from here.

Long dream about you last night. Seems we were in the Foreign Legion together, but the Legion seemed to be in Russia. I asked you how long we had been in, and you said: "A year and a half." And I groaned, thinking of the three and a half years we still had to go . . .

I enclose some routines, and a slightly amended version of the Monster Birth routine which might do for Black Mountain. I think maybe a routine and the Yage Dream, including Meet Café, might be better. Say the Baboon Huntsmen routine and the Yage Dream. But do whatever you think best. Perhaps the first chapter of Interzone . . . Please, Allen, you decide. Well, I want to get this in the mail.

Love,
Bill

Monster Birth Routine might do for Black Mountain: Robert Creeley had seen passages of Burroughs' letters and published several "Interzone" pages in his final issue *Black Mountain Review* No. 7, 1957.

66.
April 9, 1956
Tanger

Dear Allen,

Still stuck in Tanger. Most urgently need $ so please send *Junkie* money, minus your commission of course, to me right away. Preferably send in cashier check on Chase or First National. Cashing personal check depends on finding friend to guarantee it. Please, Allen, do this as soon as you can, as I am really in bad way. Writing long letter today.

Love,
Bill

P.S.   Cargo U.S. Legation as always.

[Long letter: apparently lost.]

67.
April 16, 1956
Tanger

Dear Allen,

At last I have travelling orders. I move out Tuesday to contact a Doctor MacClay in London, one of those incredibly English addresses—Queens Gate Place—So it looks like I will see some action at last. Just after I wrote you, I received $500 from my father to clean up debts and go to England. And there is plenty medicine in the *farmacías*, so I can make a comfortable, leisurely exit, and not hitting the town sick with $10 capital.

Perhaps all the delay and the failures of the past two years were necessary to show me exactly how nowhere junk is, and I can't use it if I want to do anything else.

And no more of this "one shot" routine. In a word no more junk anykind ever.

If you have already sent along the royalty check, it will be forwarded. If not, best wait till you hear from me in England. I have nothing of interest to say, just want to let you know I am on my way at last. Want to get this in mail before I leave.

> Love,
> Bill

68.
Write to this address:
May 8, 1956
44 Egerton Gardens
London S.W. 3
England

Dear Allen,

I still feel terrible. Sleep maybe 1, 2 hours at dawn. I can walk for miles and come in stumbling with fatigue but I can't sleep. The thought of sex with anyone gives me the horrors . . . Last night went to a ghastly queer party where I was pawed and propositioned by a 50-year-old Liberal M.P. I told him: "I couldn't sleep with Ganymede now, let alone you."

There has been no backsliding. No codeine, no paregoric, no nothing. Not even a sleeping pill. This time I'll make it if it kills me.

Where are you and what are you doing and when are you coming to Europe? I am torn to pieces with restlessness. The Amazon expedition is becoming an obsession with me. Of course I could easily kill a few months in Spain, Italy, and Tanger. But please let me know what the exact score is with you.

Do you have any London addresses? If so please send along. Did you send the *Junkie* money to Tanger?

The cure itself was awful. From 30 grains of M per day to 0, in 7 days. But I had a real croaker, interested in Yage, Mayan archaeology, every conceivable subject and would often come to see me at 2 A.M. and stay till 5 since he knew I couldn't sleep. Please write.

                Love,
                  Bill

69.
May 15, 1956
44 Egerton Gardens
London S.W. 3

Dear Allen,

Just received your long letter. This should reach you in plenty of time.

I am amazed and delighted to hear of your fabulous job. Would God I could get one. May try the U.S. construction companies in Spain. Publishing news is good. I have given up the idea of making money from my writing so I'm not concerned about that. Creeley can publish anything he wants for any amount or nothing. Like I say I don't care aboat the gelt angle.

I am completely recovered now, very active, able to drink. Still no interest in sex. I am physically able you dig, just not innarested. When I look at a boy nothing happens. Ratty lot of boys they got here anyhoo. Maybe when I come around to it, I want women. Maybe. London drags me like a sea anchor. I want to see bright blue sky with vultures in it. A vulture in London would be an Addams cartoon. But I won't leave until I dig what's here. Dropped Seymour a line. Hope to see him. Don't worry about chippying. I know the score now. I can't take one shot or paregoric or codeine or demerol or junk in any form. Not now or ever. If I ever have to take some for intense pain, the withdrawal syndrome can be headed off with several injections of Apomorphine. The doctor has given me 3 tubes of apomorphine to keep with me at all times. Addiction to apomorphine is impossible. It's nothing you take for kicks.

During early withdrawal vivid nightmares when I could sleep. Sample: North Africa ten years from now. A vast rubbish heap. Blue sky and hot sun. Smell of hunger and death. Smoke of petrol fires in the distance. Dave walking beside me carrying a can of gasoline. He is actually 26. In the dream he looks sixty, any age, and I know I look the same. We meet five Arabs. I see the eyes of the Arab in front and say to Dave: "Throw the petrol on them and light it! It's our only chance". Two Arabs down, covered with burning petrol (petrol is English word for gasoline. *Not kerosene.* I got in habit of using it). Other Arabs running up. We won't make it. My leg is covered with petrol. My leg is part of the dump heap. When I try to move it broken bottles and tin cans and rusty wire cut into the flesh. Someone screaming in my ear. One of a series of dreams in which I am a minority in a vast, hostile country. Finally comparative security through Public Works, complicated locks and channels and harbors and markets all synchronized with physiological calendars. In short the Natives can't use the Works without us. If they could understand the Works they would not be hostile. Someday they will maybe. But that's hundreds of years away now. Now they must use the Works and put up with us or die. An extremist party wants to destroy the Works and kill us, even if they do die. The Natives and The Work Guards (who form a separate power group) keep the extremists in line. Burning them to death when they catch them.

I just got letter from friend in Tanger. Another Arab ran Amok and cut up six Europeans. Curious fact is this:

the Arabs put the snatch on him and were getting ready to burn him alive when the police intervened.

I can't tell you how glad I am that you are coming around to accept your Harlem experience, rejecting Trilling etc. I have felt for years that this is right for you.

I can't write any more now. I am still very restless and it is a great trouble to sit down and write anything.

Love,
Bill

Your fabulous job: As yoeman-storekeeper on a Military Sea Transport ship going to Icy Cape, Alaska, thru Arctic Circle, with good pay.

Seymour: Seymour Wyse, Jack Kerouac's jazz-listening mentor and Horace Mann School chum, now had a Greenwich music shop in Chelsea, London.

70.
May 30, 1956
London

Dear Allen,

I throw in the towel. I can't stay in this fucking blighted dump another day. No wonder a man gets on power kicks here. They got no other kicks. I'd like to see the whole fucking city out in Hyde Park lined up on their hind legs begging for the chocolate I'd throw them: "These ID's can only learn a few simple tricks."

I finally found B. Mutual disinterest. I gave him your Ms., and will also arrange through Alan to send it to Auden, or better, show it to him when he comes to Italy later this Summer. You must understand London is a blighted place. Worse than Oklahoma or Texas or Quito or Bogotá, or any place I ever see in all my travels. I want to leave RIGHT NOW. No juke boxes even. Anyplace with music is under lock and key. Private club. Members only. Music is like illegal here.

Sign in pub: "No liquor may be consumed after time is called. Drinking must stop at once, NO TIME BEING ALLOWED FOR CONSUMPTION." When time is called you spit your drink out on the bar, or if you have inadvertently swallowed an illegal mouthful, you vomit it up. The establishments provide apomorphine for this purpose.

I have tried to like England but it's not possible. I'd sooner live in Hell.

What a horrible evening I spent with B. I only come back to this dump to see Elks on business.

What kind of a check you send me furthechrissakes? Made out to your landlady for Light and Rent yet. Seldom have I seen a less negotiable object.

Last night is the fucking payoff. I made an expedition to the East End to find a bar with a juke box, arriving 15 minutes before time. I mean I have travelled like to East Orange to spend ten minutes in like a Third Avenue bar. I will limp into Venice on the train without dime one. If I hadn't been waiting for that stupid bastard Seymour to show me where the action is in London, I'd been out of here five days ago with *bastante fluss*. As it was I had to put the touch on my croaker, only friend I got in this dump. Well, Seymour should ask me where the action is in Tanger or Panama or wherever. I'll give him the old Snipe Hunt Routine:

"Now, Seymour, you see this street here, Sargasso Juntion? Well, this isn't The Street. The Street runs parallel to Sargasso at an unspecified angle and sorta blends into it out past the Old Infinity Café on Eel Run Creek. Well, the Infinity was termited in 1912, and Eel Run Creek is dry as a whore's cunt on Sunday morning since the Boer War of '76, God Bless America, so when you get out beyond where The Infinity was, like as not you are on The Street. So proceed till you step into a dead whore or horse, makes no never mind like the song say, pivot sharp to *your* left. Time out to piss or whatever in the Lamprey Pissoir, and watch those Candiru. They jump two feet—Now make a complete circle to your right and swing back sixty degrees magnetic. Look for a blind beggar with two pricks one hard and one soft, it's a gimmick to arouse sympathy and generally disarm the passerby you dig? So what are you waiting for? Knock on any door whyncha, and if some one sticks his head out HE'S NOT THE MAN. Take a hydraulic lift back to The Socco and start from first principles. Is that all quite clear?

"Incidentally there's like a Connection across The River. I got it straight from a young prospector died in my arms—(He tried to fight me off but like I say he was in a weakened condition. Anyhoo I'm right strong when I get my blood up)—who had it from an Indian boy known as Standing Ass to his friends and he don't have an enemy in The Upper Amazon, who had it from a medicine man in a nutmeg trance, who had it from a rare species of talking monkey now extinct. Just here, Seymour. Wade right in and tell the piranha fish to move over."

71.
June 7, 1956
Venice

Dear Allen,

Venice is like a Mohammedan heaven with boys. I mean the one thing wrong with Venice is that it isn't quite real. Don't know exactly how long I will stay, but in no rush to move on. I got it in mind I want to go to Arabia, but it's a place they don't let you in. The family is coming on real tiresome. They say I should get a job yet, as if jobs were laying all around. Well I will try to construction companies in Spain, but from what I hear the chances are not good. Well I will think further on it. How are my chances in the Merchant Marine?

[Remainder of letter missing.]

72.
Venice
June 9 [1956]

Dear Allen,

Yours of the 28 and 31 of May received. Rexroth sounds like a real drag, I mean the whole SOUND. I already wrote you I don't click with B. or anyone else in London. What's Lucien doing on West Coast?

Alan and I are on the way to cruise the San Marco. I have not had a piecea ass in two days. The situation is desperate. No interest in junk, but alcohol may pass same in the stretch as my nemesis. Distinguished myself by getting country drunk in Peggy Guggenheim's palaccio with most deplorable results. It's like now when I walk in anywhere somebody rushes up and firmly thrusts a glass of tomato juice into my hand. Otherwise healthy as a rat, but restless like I can't sit still. I am learning to operate a gondola, swim, walk all over Venice and never want to go to bed except when I latch onto a *ragazzo*.

I will try to order some LSD6 through croaker here—friend of Alan's—Jeez I don't know what to say about the seventy dollars. Looks like it will never catch up to me.

I got a letter from Dave Lamont, friend in Tanger, he has a job lined up in Casablanca. Maybe I can get one too. Will certainly try. I am writing to Dave Lamont now. More or less I plan to be in North Africa in the late summer, but anything could happen. Like I say Venice is real gone, I mean *too much*. Such boys.

          Love,
            Bill

73.
June 18, 1956
Venice

Dear Allen,

I wrote twice to your ship address. Hope the FBI didn't intercept. I'll say it again. London is about the most Godawful place I was ever in. I never want to see England again except maybe Doc Elks on business and D. Dent. Seymour stood me up three times. He should look me up somewhere sometime, and I'll do as much for him. I did give Barker your Ms., but did not see him again to get reaction.

Venice is perhaps the greatest place I ever see. Such a cornucopia of available young ass. I mean too much. Since the cure I been sexy as an eighteen-year-old and healthy as a rat. Row or operate gondola for 2 or 3 hours every day. Also swim. Rest of the time chasing after the *ragazzi*. Difficult to get any work done here. However I am planning a nightmare tour of Europe entitled THE GRAND TOUR—(HELL IS WHERE YOUR ASS IS), of which I enclose beginning of Scandinavian chapter. This was inspired by a Swede I met at party, a cured alcoholic who told me in Sweden drug addicts are chained—*chained* yet—to the bed and left there until cured—or dead. I begin to suspect that all is not well behind that hygienic Scandinavian facade.

Alan is writing you. Incidentally I got country drunk

in Peggy Guggenheim's palaccio, in consequence forever banished from her premises. In fact I have managed to alienate quite a number of people by my drunken behavior which can, I realize, be rather difficult to take. Well I'm not a bit alarmed about that. One thing is sure I'm really off the junk now, but would like to pick up on some weed. They got like a connection in Padua, an old bitch in a tenement that smells like black market cigarettes. Looks like set for Italian movie or Horne Burns novel.

Interesting about your mother's improvement. I have thought a great deal about Schizophrenia (S in the trade). Convinced that it is as much a disease of disturbed metabolism as diabetes. In my opinion psychological treatment is not only worthless but absolutely contraindicated, certainly while the disease process is in operation. I have revised my earlier theory which I outlined to you (anxiety produced adrenaline, which produces histamine both H and A break down into the S substance—recently isolated from the blood of S's—which in turn produces more H and A). The S substance must be produced by the body for an excellent biological reason, perhaps to *counteract* the metabolic products of anxiety. Now I have frequently observed that there are no psychotic junkies, at least not when on the junk. (Patient of Dent who was in nuthouse for alcoholism complicated by psychosis—undiagnosed—He was violent and hallucinating—So they gave him morphine, he became addicted and was discharged from the hospital cured of alcoholism and psychosis but on the junk. Then some croaker gave him demerol to get him off morphine and he came to Dr. Dent with a demerol habit—one of the worst if you ask me and I'm the man who should know—So Dent makes with the apomorphine treatment—note apomorphine as back-brain stimulant and general regulator of disturbed metabolism—and when I meet this character he is fully dressed and in his right mind cured of demerol, alcoholism and psychosis.) Now fix yourself on this: the terminal state of addiction is quite similar to the terminal state of S. Complete destruction of affect, withdrawal, etc. I used to spend six hours looking at my shoe. Seymour knows heroin addict who spends his whole life in bed, even shits there when he shits, if he shits. But here is crucial difference between deteriorated S and terminal addict (by a terminal addict I mean one who gets all he wants). The T.A. will get up off his piles on the double if his junk is cut. With suitable withdrawal treatment he will be his normal pre-junk self in a month. His sickness *is* H. Possibly S is quite similar. If the body produced its own H until tolerance and withdrawal syndrome was established and then continued to produce it to prevent withdrawal syndrome, we would have analogy of S process as I tentatively see it. So I say give S's H for some months until addiction is established, then a withdrawal treatment with apomorphine. If that doesn't work, try giving LSD6 sub—and maybe the body getting it from outside will stop producing, and the S substance can be withdrawn like junk. I tell you with a free hand I could get all the S's out on the street collecting unemployment compensation.

    The family is making tiresome sounds like things are tough and I should get a job. Investigating possibilities of work in Spain and Casablanca. *A ver*. I had letter from Jack. I will write him presently. The $70 went to London, but will be forwarded here.

P.S.   I am 42 but feel like eighteen. Also act that way. Will send first chapter of HELL IS WHERE YOUR ASS IS later. Enclose instead latest routine.

address c/o U.S. Consulate
Venice, Italy

74.
Sept. 13, 1956
Tanger, Morocco
c/o U.S. Consulate

Dear Allen,

This writing finds me languid and sate, after a *divine* siesta *à deux, à trois* actually: Myself; the inevitable Arab boy, 18 and willowy, darling with a skiiinnn like the inside of an oyster shell; and, of course, that ubiquitous old voyeur bitch Miss Green. By the lay, my fanny is back in combat, you might say if you were a type citizen to say a thing like that. How's this for an ad: "You too can be screwed by a brace of Nubians and feel *noooooo* pain . . . Amazing new remedy will put your ass back in action . . . MA LEE'S PILE GOOK . . ."

I have so much to communicate it would constitute a trilogy. Can only hit a few headlines. I left Venice August 10 and proceeded from Naples to Tripoli. Tripoli utter nowhere. Fraternizing between Arabs and Europeans is literally spat upon. I mean the Arabs spit on the sidewalk when you pass and yell: "Cock suck Mericans go home." A German in Tripoli told me: "The Arabs are bad now". Like the weather. Living in Arab territory is like living in the cyclone belt. You see Arabs—pronunced A-rabs—is bad to riot. You don't have to mind one A-rab or like a small group, but let a thousand of them connive together and wig collective, they can really come on evil. So Tripoli got like segregation imposed by the A-rabs, besides which it is ugly, and *hot* my *God*. So I proceed to Algiers where the civil war is in progress . . . (The other day an Arab who had thrown a bomb into a café was torn to pieces by an infuriated crowd of French, and this in downtown Oran. Unhappily I was not there to see it. Anyone throws a bomb in a café or cinema deserves to be strewn over Deaf Smith County Texas, stap my vitals.) Sample conversation between your reporter and a nameless Arab Asshole:

A.A.: "Hey, Johnny, feelthy pictures?"

LEE: "No."
A.A.: See me fuck sister? Me rimmy you?"
LEE: "No." (walking away)
A.A.: "Fuck you son bitch. Go back to your own country . . ."

In short, to deal plainly, I am definitely anti the Arab Nationalists and pro-French so far as the Algerian setup goes. You can't imagine what a pain in the ass these Nationalists are. Bastards, sons a bitches . . .

Tanger is all right now, but subject to change at any time. The A-rabs is attempting to enforce a sexual blockade on the Unbelievers. Anyone known to fraternize is subject to reprisals. My boy that just left was kidnapped and thrown out of a car and sustained a broken leg to sanction his liaison with an English tourist. It looks to me like the Westerners are getting the slow toe. Meanwhile Tanger is better than ever but jittery. "The hour darkens and grows always later." . . . I am staying here until or unless I have to leave . . . Spain is right over yonder. Cheap and teeming with the young amenities stap my vitals . . . Your picture of Stateside sexual mores is too ghastly. You simply must immerse yourself in this Fountain of Youths . . . But even in Moslem Heaven, stocked with beautiful Arab fingerlings, Bum Kicks stalk the golden streets twanging discordant harps . . . The other night I made it with a boy I have known off and on, in and out you might say, for three years . . . in fact he was my first Tanger piece. Well after the ball was over, he wants to stay all night and stay a little longer . . . and I indicate as tactfully as such a concept can be effectively indicated that I considered this project inconvenient in the widest sense . . . So he says: "All right. I'll go. All right. Just remember I'm always your friend . . . Always there if you want me . . . I can wait." And another one has been following me around for three days. Everytime I look up, there he is about twenty feet away. Just waiting, just sitting, just hanging around and don't say nothing. Now some stupid ass holes think it would be excruciatingly chic to own a sure-nuff boy slave. Maybe. At first. Six months later there he is, in an old creaky rocking chair especially designed for certain sexual practices—Must I draw a blue print?—just a-setting and a-rocking . . .

"Why don't you *go* some place?"

"Got no place to go, massa, nothing to do but wait on your pleasure . . ." Creak, creak, creak.

Three months later . . . Look I *give* you your freedom . . ."

"Can't take freedom off you, massa, any more than your hand could take freedom."

Creak, creak, creak . . .

Three months later . . ."I'll give you every cent I have and live with my sainted mother the old cunt if you'll only go."

"Don't need money, massa." Creak, creak, creak . . .

"What do you want of me?"

"You do the wanting, massa." Creak, creak, creak . . .

You recall my dream about throwing gasoline on Arabs and lighting it? I have had an even more sinister sequel. I was in a café like. An old man appeared in a doorway, a short old man with a gray face and a grey beard. He makes no move, says nothing. I have a pewter jug of boiling acid in my hand. Possessed by a convulsive urgency of hate and fear, I throw the acid into his face . . . You read about Telvi, of course, the jerk who threw acid in Reisel's face? And you recall my dream about the Holy Man who was making with a Malignant Telepathic Broadcast? Tel-Vi. This was the Holy Man. I am developing Holy Man concept in Interzone. Latest Control Concepts: Anyone using telepathy as means of coercion must cut himself off from all protoplasmic contacts. He must always send, but never receive . . . He becomes an automaton, a ventriloquist dummy, withers in orgoneless limbo. But I don't have time to go into all my latest concepts on Control, Schizophrenia, Junk, Cancer . . . I have a theory that no one with schizophrenia has cancer, that the two conditions are metabolically incompatible. If you know a croaker and get to it, just ask him to check the cause of death in schizos . . . I must wait till I see you. Well if you can pick up another $500 better do it. About sleeping bags I dunno. I am all against the Russian expedition. You would not be allowed to travel like that. You do it Intourist or you don't do it, and that costs minimum $20 per day. Fuck that sound. Try to get a boat to Gibraltar or Barcelona. Best take the U.S. Export to Gibraltar. If the situation here takes a sticky turn we can arrange to meet in Spain.

Where is Jack? Give him my love, and also to Neal or anybody else. Plenty to go round you might say. I was pleased by Whalen's comments on my work . . .

So come along to Europe, Allen, and have a good time with the boys. I can wait. But just remember I'll always be there if you want me . . . creak, creak, creak . . .

Love,
Bill

P.S. Mystic experiences lately. Non-verbal. Impossible convey, but real gone. You know I wouldn't touch even a codeine pill or a goofball. The whole idea of junk is downright repugnant to me. Sexy as an eighteen-year-old. If I don't make it every other day I am physically uncomfortable. Of course no one masturbates in Tanger. You can describe those Abstinence Kicks to me. I'll get them vicarious, contact kicks you might say . . .

    Typical Tanger conversation: A bunch of the boys preparing to start on hike with picnic lunch . . . "We are subject to be set upon and raped by Arabs. Be sure to bring along your K.Y., dahling."

    Emmett, who looks and talks like a typical retired American businessman, says in flat Midwest accent: "They have to move fast to rape me." . . .

A charming young queer English boy from
Oxford just left. I think maybe I was too hasty about
England. Hmmmmm . . .

I will drop Carl a line . . . Keep me posted on
your plans. Yes, I received the $70 in Venice
. . . Thanks . . .

Address here is: Cargo U.S. Consulate
                 Tanger, Morocco

The Legation has moved to Rabat.

I can fix you up with the son of a local Cad, I mean
Caid, of course, for $10. Like the song say, "He will do
it anytime" etc.

Bastards, sons a bitches: A paraphrase of a classic line
Burroughs remembered from Kells Elvins' father whom he
described as suffering advanced paretic psychopathy. Same
lines used in *So Proudly We Hail*.

Reisel: Victor Reisel, a N.Y. labor columnist who was
blinded by an acid attack after he attacked organized crime
infiltration of labor unions.

Whalen's comments: Philip Whalen, reading Bill's letters
in Milvia St. cottage, Berkeley, had been delighted by Bill's
vivid prose.

75.
Sept. 16, 1956
Tanger, Morrocco

Dear Allen,

Just got your letter so will expect you and entourage
January. 'Tis I'll be here in sunshine or in shadow like the
song say (unless they are giving me the hard toe). There
is no town like Tanger town. The place relaxes me so I
am subject to dissolve. I can spend three hours looking at
the bay with my mouth open like a Kentucky Mountain
Boy. Man, I don't *need* junk. Speaking of which, I never
feel the slightest temptation. I think junkies relapse
because they are not *metabolically* cured by the usual

methods of treatment. Dent's apomorphine method could dispose of the whole problem.

This you gotta hear: There is a Holy Man around town who tells fortunes in his spare time from being a Holy Man. So an English woman consults the old fuck and he tells her: "Lady, you want to get my potent virtue from the living source," hauling out the living source. "Lunch on it, sister, and do yourself some good. I'm giving you the chance extraordinary." The routines some citizens put down.

I never been so horny in my life as right lately. Like yesterday I had two-hour set–to with Nimón, my latest heart-throb—that's a way of putting it. So today I should be thinking about higher things. So what I do all afternoon? Lounge about in my wine-colored Czechoslovakian Poplin pyjamas devising Rube Goldberg sex contraptions: like an ingenious assortment of rocking chairs and sofas that rock back and forth and sideways, not to mention Ma Lee's Special: the rocking swivel chair guaranteed to run up casualties among the Saturday-night lush trade; vibrating mattresses, innaresting hammocks, facilities in scenic railways and stunting planes
. . . currently working on an arrangement involving aqualungs and a blood-temperature swimming pool with artificial waves.

Spot of landlady bother. She tells me to slack off on the Arab visitors. So me and Dave, the Walter Winchell of Tanger, have found us the original anything-goes joint. Run by a retired madame from Saigon. On the ground floor will be Dave, myself and Eric the Public School Man (Eton 26), who conspired with a male hustler to forge a stolen traveller check. The boy brought the deal to me first and I told him "I should felonize myself for $25?? What you think I am, a crook? Take that business to Eric." So they got by with it I hope. You never know. The mills of American Express grind slow but they grind exceeding fine. One of these days a man in a grey flannel suit (the bastards come on elegant these days making so much money) is likely to tap Eric on the shoulder and say: "Are you Eric Trevor-Orme-Smith-Creighton also known as 'El Chinche' (The Bed Bug)?" Anyhoo we three occupy the ground floor with our rooms opening on the garden and have a private entrance: "You can be *free* here, you understand?" the old whore says to me digging me in the ribs. The houseboy is a Spanish queer, good-looking in a depraved sort of way. I don't often use the word but no other word gets the job done: that boy has one of the most degenerate faces I ever saw. When you hear one of the whores screaming "Joselito! Joselito!" you know Joselito is laying one of the clients again. Eric throws a fuck into him when he gets caught short. So it's like a goodly crowd is there you might say.

A strange thing happened this morning. I was doing my special abdominal exercises I learned from a citizen named Hornibrook in London who learned them from the Fiji Islanders near as I can make out. So suddenly a wave of sex come over me and I have a spontaneous orgasm stap my vitals. Now a spontaneous waking orgasm is a rare occurrence even in adolescence. Only one I ever experienced before was in the orgone accumulator I made in Texas. And another thing. I find my eyes straying towards the fair sex. (Its the new *frisson*, dearie . . . Women are downright piquant.) You hear about these old characters find out they are queer at fifty, maybe I'm about to make with the old switcheroo. What are these strange feelings that come over me when I look at a young cunts, little tits sticking out so cute? Could it be that?? No! No! He thrust the thought from him in horror . . . He stumbled out into the street with the girl's mocking laughter lingering in his ears, laughter that seemed to say "Who you think you're kidding with the queer act? I know you, baby." Well, it is as Allah wills . . .

I am writing now a straight continuation of Interzone. If you are going to be around a bit I will send along the second chapter when I get it finished which will be very soon. Maybe I can publish with Obelisk Press in Paris. Alan didn't say anything about this deal to publish *Naked*

Lunch in Paris. Well *a ver, a ver* . . . If you have a copy of *Time* article on *Howl* I would love to see it. What issue? We get it here eventually in the American Library . . .

My best to Jack, Neal, Corso. I will write Jack in Mexico.

They got like half-assed gondolas I row around every day. Physical exercise, the contracting and relaxing of muscles, is for me an exquisite sensual pleasure . . . So, things give me pleasure, walking around town, sitting in a café. I have no compulsion to write or to do anything except when I am possessed by routines, which can happen any time. A lot of the time I just sit blank and narcotized, letting sensations flow through me. I have a feeling that I might turn into somebody else, that I am losing my outlines. A curious illusion I get lately when I am a little lushed and swing on Miss Green's unnatural tit, I feel that there is another person present. I mean like the last time I laid Ahmed (he is being the most "sincere"—advertising agency argot for somebody all out on the make—male hustler in Greater Tanger and is sensational, uninhibited sex. The things that boy thinks up to do!). So I feel like there is a Third Man in the room. Not disapproving or anything. Just there. At times I feel myself on the verge of something incredible, like I will meet myself on the way out. This extra person kick has happened several times. And I don't really need Miss Green any more . . .

The English boy was talking about suicide, life not worth living. This seems incredible to me. I think I must be very happy. I got like a Revelation but can't verbalize it. Let me know when you are going etc.

       Love,
       Bill

P.S. Address Cargo U.S. Consultate
   Tanger, Morocco
   The Legation has moved to Rabat

76.
13 Oct. 1956
[Tanger]

Dear Allen,

I don't see our roles reversed exactly but expanded and altered on both sides. I have entered a period of change more drastic than adolescence or early childhood. I live in a constant state of routine. I am getting so far out one day I won't come back at all. I can't take time to go into all my mystic experiences which I have whenever I walk out the door. There is something special about Tanger. It is the only place when I am there I don't want to be anyplace else. No stasis horrors here. And the beauty of this town that consists in changing combinations. Venice is beautiful, but it never changes. It is a dream congealed in stone. And it is someone else's dream. The final effect is to me nightmarish—Example: sky supersonic, orgone blue, warm wind, a stone stairway leading up to the Old Town . . . Coming down the stairs a very dark Arab boy with a light purple shirt . . .

I get average of ten very attractive propositions a day. My latest number is Spanish, 16, with a smile hit you right in the nuts. I mean that pure, uncut boy stuff, that young male innocence . . . American boys are not innocent because they lack experience. Innocence is inseparable from depravity. You can lay him when you get here. Everyone else has . . . That child innocence but what technique and virtuosity. Oh la la . . . Now I got myself agitated—must have him today instead of tomorrow . . . Incidentally the one reason I get so many propositions is I am being the most eligible queer in Greater Tanger. Everyone knows how generous I was with Kiki. And I got a rep for being a perfect gentleman in every sense of the word.

I work when I can sit still long enough, or when I get time out from fucking. Actually Interzone has taken complete shape. If I only had a tape recorder I could finish it in a month. Enclose selections which will indicate where I am. Finale is they set off a new atom bomb at the Fourth of July celebration and destroy the world . . . Getting quite friendly with Paul Bowles. He is really a charming person . . . New Quarters are superb. My room opens onto a garden, no maids to bother me . . . A private entrance on a quiet street . . . I don't see how anyone could be happier than I am right now . . . I mean this is it . . . I am not saving myself for anything . . . I hope to God I don't have to leave Tanger . . . Of course the South of Spain is terrific . . . They are all Republicans even the fuzz . . . The old folks sit in the kitchen drinking wine while you lay their boy in the bedroom. Nice, informal atmosphere, you dig . . . I mean I won't exactly be withering on the vine if I do have to leave . . . But Tanger is my dream town. I did have a dream ten years ago of coming into a harbor and knowing that this was the place where I desired to be . . . Just the other day, rowing around in the harbor I recognized it as my dream bay.

I wish you would come on here before you fritter away your loot. By all means bring Jack and Peter. I assure you I will not be jealous . . . In fact jealousy is one of the emotions of which I am no longer capable. Self-pity is also impossible for me. You know what is wrong with it? Self-pity is a symptom of a divided ego, split into a pitied and a pitier. If your ego is intact, you *can't* pity yourself . . . I discovered this in a state of complete despair a few days ago. I woke up one morning to find that my ass and environs was a bright purple red color—overtook by my nemesis you might say . . . So after a session with medical books in the Red Cross, I was *convinced* I had that awful virus veneral disease Lymphogranuloma—where your ass turns purple and seals up, only deigning to emit an occasional purulent discharge . . . I went home and dosed myself with antibiotics—that disease is difficult to cure though Aureomycin has proved effective in some cases. Then I

began to cry and roll around, biting my knuckles in complete despair. Despair unifies the ego. Self-pity is impossible . . . Did you know that tears rid the body of poisonous wastes, like sweat or urine? In jaundice your tears are bright yellow. In short, grief or despair causes metabolic poisons to accumulate. The old idea that someone who is greatly afflicted must cry or die has a sound metabolic basis. Anyhoo I never seen anyone take on the way I did for hours and hours, repeating over and over "Take it away—Take it away." So the next day I go to the doctor, he takes a look and purses his lips and says: "Yes you have rather a severe case of ringworm . . . athletes foot . . ." Then he looked at me over his glasses and smiled discreetly . . . "And there seems to have been a certain amount of uh chafing." So I used Mycocten and my ass is no longer purple
. . . Seems to me I got my despair revelations at bargain basement price. I mean the self-pity insight was only one angle. Another was I found out how emphatically I disapprove of stealing or any criminal activities . . . I mean criminal, not illegal . . whether performed by criminals or by police or by anybody. That is, crimes against property and person of others: brainwashing, thought control, etc., is the vilest form of crime against the person of another. There is no greater disaster than the confusion of ethics and legality. It is the curse of the Western World, the substitution of law—that is, force —for instinctive feeling for others. Once this is done, on the one hand anything legal is right and such monstrosities as Nazism and Communism are loosed on the world, on the other hand anything you can get by with is all right too, which is the lesser, because self-limiting, evil of ordinary criminality. Only America could have set up such a perversion as the concept that the good are dull and the wicked charming. Al Capp says "Good is better than evil because it is nicer." I say it's better because it's more interesting. Evil is dull, about as glamorous as a cancer. And evil men are dull—as I am sure Himmler was dull.

But I doubt that I could ever have learned this in the States. And I used to admire gangsters. Good God. I remember seeing in the paper those gangsters who conspired to throw acid in Reisel's face and thinking quite spontaneously "What a bunch of shits they are."

Well I was never one to beat around inna bush. I mean enough of this silly lovemaking, take off your clothes . . . Al, I am a fucking saint, that is, I been fucked by the Holy Ghost and knocked up with the Immaculate Woid . . . I'm the third coming, me, and don't know if I can do it again . . . So stand by for the Revelation . . .

Christ? That cheap mountebank, the bushleaguer. You think I'd demean myself to commit a miracle? That's what Christ shoulda said onna Cross when the citizens said "Make with a miracle and save your own ass." He shoulda said "I wouldn't demean myself. The show must go on." He always was one to miss a cue . . .

I recall when we was doing an Impersonation act in Sodom and that is one cheap town. Strictly from hunger . . . Well this citizen, this fuckin' Philistine who wandered in from Podunk Baal or some place, calls me a fuckin' fruit right onna floor . . . And I said to him "Three thousand years in show business and I always keep my nose clean . . . Besides I don't hafta take any shit off any uncircumcised cock sucker." Like I say, miracles is the cheapest trick inna industry. Some people got no class to them. That one shoulda stood in carny. "Step right up Marks and Marquessa and bring the little Marks too, good for young and old, man and beast, the one and only legit Son of Man will cure a young boy's clap with one hand—by contact alone folks—create marijuana with the other whilst walking on water and squirtin' wine out his ass . . . Now don't crowd too close . . . You are subject to be irradiated by the sheer charge of this character . . ."

Buddha? A notorious metabolic junky. Makes his own you dig. In India where they got no sense of time The Man is often a month late. "Now let me see is that the second or third monsoon? I got like a meet in Ketchipur about more or less."

So you dig these junkies sittin' around in the lotus posture waitin on the Man.

So Buddha says: "I don't hafta take this sound. I'll by God metabolize my own junk."

"Man, you cant do that. The revenooers will swarm all over you."

"No they won't. I got a gimmick see? I'm a fuckin' Holy Man as of now on out."

"Jeez, Boss, what an angle."

"Now some citizens when they make with the New Religion really wig . . . No class to them . . . Besides they is subject to be lynched because who wants somebody hanging around being better than other folks? 'What you want to do, Jack, give people a bad time?' So we gotta play it cool, you dig, cool . . . We got a take-it-or-leave-it proposition here folks. We aren't shoving anything up your soul, unlike certain cheap characters who shall be nameless and are nowhere . . . These frantic citizens don't know how to come on."

Mohammed? Are you, kiddin'? He was dreamed up by the Mecca Chamber of Commerce. An Egyptian ad man onna skids from the sauce wrote the continuity . . .

"I'll have one more, Gus. Then I'll by God go home and receive a Surah . . . Wait till the morning edition hits the Souks. I'm blasting Amalgamated wide open."

"Give em Hell, Kid, I'm in your corner."

"Gus, when the roll is called up yonder you'll be there if I hafta louse up the Universe . . . I won't forget you Gussie . . . I won't forget what you done for me . . ."

"*Wait* a minute, wait a *minute*. That'll be ten clams . . . in cash . . ."

Confucius . . . Who he?

Lao Tze . . . They scratch him already . . .

So now we got the place cleaned up a bit, I'm gonna make with the Living Word . . .

Everybody in this fuckin' curved universe and anybody

say it's not curved is blaspheming The Immaculate Fact and the first prophet of Fact, Einstein—one of my stooges you dig . . . Everybody and everything is in this universe together . . . If one explodes we all explode . . . That Thermodynamic drag brings everybody down . . . Fuck your nabor . . . He may like it . . . And I want you fellows to control your most basic instinct, which is the yen to control, coerce, violate, invade, annihilate, by any means whatsoever, anybody else's physical or psychical person . . . Anybody wants to go climb into someone else and take over is no better than a fuckin' control addict. He should kick his noisome habit instead of skulking around with his bare ass hanging out lousing up the Universe . . . Be it known that such nameless ass holes will suffer a painful doom. And remember, when the control yen rips through your bones like a great black wind you have connected for Pure Evil . . . Not the glamorous bitch, but the cancerous, rotting Drag who says "I have nothing to offer but my sores . . ." So when you feel that yen, brother, and everybody in the industry must feel it, and say "How can I make it without the stuff," It and the universe will rush in with The Immaculate Fix . . . and you will look The Man straight in his disks—power pushers don't need eyes—and say "Gimpy take up thy shit and walk." Go on the nod and dream of a square universe, I stand with THE FACTS.

   I mean enough of these gooey Saints with that look of pathic dismay as if they were being fucked and pretending not to pay it any mind. He who denies himself will shit sure deny others . . . Leave us have no more square saints . . . Get a typewriter whyncha? This letter is like a Mayan codice. Neither of you writes good anyhoo. It reads like the Drunken Newscaster . . . remember? . . . at last a sentence I can read . . . Yes Peter, I live on a hill overlooking the bay in the most beautiful city in the world or at least it's always young and fair to me . . . You got cockroaches . . . Well I wake up this morning with rat shit on my sheets . . . I am subject to be took advantage of by rats . . . When I lived in the other house I useta get my exercise killing rats with a cane in the patio . . . the bastards eat babies you dig so I put them to the sword or whatever . . . No compromise with the unbelieving pricks . . . Now I haven't issued a Surah on cockroaches yet since there are none here . . . You boys will just have to piece out the odds without you know The Last Word on roaches . . . Want to talk to you about the nuthouse, schizophrenia being like one of my hobbies you might say and I got theories about it like I got about most everything. Don't be responsible Peter . . . That sentence sounds like you was applying for a position . . . You know the routines citizens put down . . . like "I am a young man with clean habits. I don't juice and I don't mainline" . . . If what's on my mind is on your mind, you must be kid simple . . . If so, you are coming to the right place . . . Now look here, don't worry about my sensitiveness . . . There'll be no Indian rope trick put down . . . Nobody disappears in Tanger . . . Now look I feel a Surah coming on the subject of roaches . . . I mean you gotta draw the line someplace. Like I should go around with a purple ass I don't want to kill them cute little ringworms already? They has committed an unspeakable crime in violating my person without so much as a by your leave . . . Germs got no class to them. And the evilest of them all are the virus . . . So bone lazy they aren't even hardly alive yet . . . Fuckin transitional bastards . . . So I say cockroaches can live for all I care but not in my quarters. I didn't send for no cockroaches . . . They is invading my privacy and I by God won't stand still for it . . . The prophet has yacked . . . I'm off to this restaurant where all the waiters and the cook are Arabian fruits who keep feeling up the clientele . . . Sign over the bar: "Employees must wash hands after goosing the clients."

    Enclose samples of Interzone . . . This is first rough draft . . . I have written about fifty pages . . . A boy last night and another this noon . . . I am declaring a two-day sex Lent,

>>Bless you My Children,
>>>Love from
>>>>Pop Lee Your Friendly Prophet
>>>Bill

DON'T GO TO MEXICO . . . COME RIGHT HERE RIGHT NOW WHILE YOU HAVE THE LOOT. TANGER IS THE PLACE . . . WHY WAIT . . . ???

It reads like the Drunken Newscaster: A BBC broadcast, the tape of which recording engineer Jerry Newman had played for Burroughs in 1953, N.Y.—"Princess Margaret spent the night inside her parents at Balmoral Castle." The Drunken Newscaster inspired many Burroughs routines.

77.
Oct 29, 1956
Tanger

Dear Allen,

Pick out whatever you like for *Cambridge Review*, and bring Ms. with you when you come. I really got the juice up on Interzone and it will be finished by Xmas. I am working at least four hours a day Possible finale: Anal technician pulls the switch that blows up the world: "They'll hear this fart on Jupiter."

This town really has the *jihad* jitters—*jihad* means the wholesale slaughter by every Moslem of every unbeliever. Yesterday I am sitting in the Socco and suddenly people start running and all the shop keepers are slamming down the steel shutters of their shops—I plan to market an automatic shop closer whereby you press a button and your shutter falls like a guillotine—and everybody in the cafés drops their drinks and leaps inside and the waiters are closing the doors. So at this point about thirty little children carrying the Moroccan flag troop through the Socco . . . A few days ago we had a general strike. Everything closed, restaurants, drug stores, no cars allowed on the streets. About four P.M. I am out with my Spanish kid trying to score for a bottle of cognac, and everybody says "No! Go away! Don't you know there's a strike on?" and slams the door. About this time such a racket breaks out like I never hear and I can see thousands of Arabs marching down the boulevard yelling. So I cut by police headquarters, where about a hundred young Arabs are yelling at the cops, who have barricaded themselves inside. What had happened, this idiot Frenchman climbed into a tree and harangued the crowd: "How dare you say anything against La France." Fortunately the police succeeded in rescuing him, and they had him locked in the station—On the boulevard I dig about 20,000 Arabs, mostly teen-agers, yelling *"Fuera Français!"* (Out with the French!) and jumping around and laughing . . . So nothing happened . . . Tell Jack not to worry about a thing.

As to my house it is one room and one bed generally cluttered up with Spanish boys. The sexual mores here unlike anything you can imagine. So long as I go with Spanish boys, it is like having a girl in the U.S. I mean you feel yourself at one with society. No one disapproves or says anything. Whereas to walk around town with an Arab boy would be unthinkable at this point. You would be insulted, stared at, spit at, and the boy would be subject to reprisals. You dig no one cares what the unbelievers do among themselves. I have a strange feeling here of being outside any social context. I have never known anyplace so relaxing. The possibility of an all-out riot is like a tonic, like ozone in air: "here surely is a song for men like wind in an iron tree"—*Anabasis* more or less. I have no nostalgia for the old days in Morocco, which I never saw. Right now is for me.

My disregard of social forms is approaching psychosis. Drinking with some very stuffy English people on their yacht and someone says something about someone tied to a buoy, and I say "Tied to a boy? Lucky chap" and sit there doubled over with laughing, completely knocked out by my own wit. I can assure you no one else thought it was a bit funny. Now when they see me they get a *sauve qui peut* look and take off on the double, probably thinking "Here comes that dangerous old fruit." So about two weeks ago I am having tea with Paul Bowles and he is entertaining this rich American woman. So I was talking about Yage, and she says "How long does it take to rot you?" and I said: "Lady you should live so long" and she left the room. So I thought that finishes me with Bowles but nothing of the sort, and I have seen him twice since, and dig him like I never dig anyone that quick before. Our minds similar, telepathy flows like water. I mean there is something portentously familiar about him, like a revelation. I also borrowed and read his book which I think very good . . . Unfortunately he is leaving for Ceylon in a few days. He will be back here in February I think, so you will probably see him.

Yes I have typewriter which I won and a good one . . . These Black Mountain cats sound like too much of rather a bad thing . . . You shouldn't be put off base by those puerile tactics. It's one of the oldest routines in the Industry. I mean distracting, or rather engaging your attention with one hand while he hits you with the other. The counterpunch? I could suggest a dozen. Like say: "Of course the only writing now is in scientific journals" and read him something about the use of antihemoglobin treatment in the control of multiple degenerative granuloma . . . Further rules: Never answer him directly, never ask what he means, just nod as if everything he was saying was rather obvious and tiresome and talk always to someone on one side of or behind him, and then fall into long silences as if listening carefully to this invisible person, nodding at intervals you dig and interjecting like "Well I wouldn't go that far. At least not yet." Or: "You *can* say that again, but it's uncalled-for really." You dig, you are discussing him with this phantom cat he has apparently brought with him into the room . . . I can't explain all this . . . It's like the sight of someone about to flip or someone full of paranoid hate excites me. I want to see what will happen if they really wig. I want to crack them wide open and feed on the wonderful soft stuff that will ooze out. When an Arab looks at me with insane hate, I hope maybe he will come apart for me so I can see the bare bones of human process spill right out under the Moroccan blue sky . . . You see a paranoid has to have the other half, that is, he must have complementary fear or hate. If I could get him to leap on me without I feel any answering fear or hate, he might crack wide open and God knows what would crawl out . . . Kicks, man, kicks . . . I mean it's like a yen . . . Jack must not be afraid of Arabs. I am in the position to officially abolish fear.

The chaos in Morocco is beautiful. Arab hipsters are developing in Casablanca, and a vast underworld. The police drive around in jeeps, machine-gunning each other . . . Where does Rexroth get off at, he has been attacked by juvenile delinquents inna soda fountain? Anyhoo it sounds like an old maid story to me.

This letter is like for you and Jack and Peter. Now listen. I will have the prologue of Interzone which is about fifty pages complete in a few weeks. Should I send you a copy? And if so where? What I am writing now supercedes, in fact makes absolete, anything I have written hitherto. Write me on this point. I am really *writing* Interzone now, not writing about it . . .

Enclose picture of Spanish boy who has quit his job and left home and moved in with me. Not, my dear, an unmixed blessing. The chorus of guides and queens in the Socco has passed it along: "Tell Willy The Junk he is asking for it, shacking with that Spanish kid who is always in hassles with the fuzz." This kid has been arrested many times for such offenses as playing ball in the street, breaking windows with his slingshot, and hitting his girl friend in public and two teeth fall out already—loose anyhoo I think and she is just making capital of her pyorrhea, four out of five get it before forty like the ad man say . . . I mean I'm a creative artist, I gotta have some privacy instead of which boys is crawling all over me at any hour at all.

   I got a great idea. A number called the Jihad Jitters . . . Start is we hear riot noises in the distance . . . ever hear it? It's terrific . . . You wouldn't believe such noises could result from humans, all sorts of strange yips . . . Then the sound of shop shutters slamming down . . . Then the vocal comes on . . . You dig, various characters who got the Jihad Jitters . . . Like first comes on this fag:
>"The Istaqal hates me,
>The guides all berates me,
>I'm nobody's sweetheart now . . .
>I mean scared of those critters,
>They's a-coming for to disembowel me"

Then comes on this English contrabandist:
>"I just wanna make a buck
>So now I gotta duck,
>and leave my bundle stand
>inna bank?
>I'll stay and take my chances
>With the bloody fucking nances,
>Jihad you can't jitter me . . ."

Now comes on a retired Colonel:
>"I've been through this before
>From Belfast to Singapore
>And I jolly well know the old score
>A native's like a horse
>Respectin' only force . . .
>So call out the Queen's Sixty-ninth . . ."

And now a Syrian Greek who peddles second-hand condoms in the souks and does a spot of feelthy tattooing on the side:

"You boys all know me
The friendly little gee,
Who keeps the bugs offen your meat
And where'd you be without the rubber
When you don't wanta club her
You got enough events as it is?"
Well you dig other types too. I'll have to give it thought.
So finally all the voices together, and mixed with the riot noises like.

"Can't you see the Lady doesn't *want* that knife? Wait here, honey face, I'm going to call the manager."

"Roy! That old nigger is lookin' at me so nasty!"

"How dare you throw gasoline on me. I'm going to call a cop." (Alt: "How dare you stick a knife up my ass? I'll . . . I'll, why I'll call a cop!")

"I say, these blighters don't look like members to me?"

And the music will be Arab, jazz, strains of the old Marseillaise, old Berber tunes etc. . . .

Really rioting must be the greatest, like (*snap*) WOW. I mean I dug it watching them Arabs jumping around yelling and laughing, and they laugh in serious riots. We laugh when anxiety is aroused and then abruptly relieved . . . Now a riot is, for the participants, a classical anxiety situation: that is, the complete surrender of control to the id . . . But this surrender is condoned: laughter.

I was looking at this Wildblood book *Against the Law*—he was one of the people convicted with Lord Montague of homosex practices . . . These English . . . The prosecutor keeps saying like "These citizens been consorting with their social inferiors . . . I suspect them to be fairies."

See an upper-class Englishman with a lamp: "Looking for an inferior . . . Like a spot of fun you know . . . ."

I have purchased a machete. If they stage a jihad I'm gonna wrap myself in a dirty sheet and rush out to do some jihading of my own like "I comma Luigi. I killa everybody." I say it's nothing but a half-assed jihad that confines itself to Unbelievers; "Let petty kings the names of parties know; Wherever I come I kill both friend and foe." Like there's this awful queer guide here name of Charley who keeps insulting poor Dave on the street, saying: "Just wait. We're going to take care of you fucking American queers." So comes the jihad I will scream "Death to the queers!" and rush up and cut Charley's head off. And I will shit sure avail myself of the next jihad to take care of the nabor's dog, the bastard is barking all night. I mean them suicidal Black Mountain boys should dig Islam already. What a beautiful way to commit suicide, to get yourself torn in pieces by Arabs. Like (*snap*) WOW. A few suggestions: Rush into a mosque, pour a pail of garbage on the floor, then make with a hog call—to coincide of course with the call to prayer —whereupon a herd of hogs you have posted nearby rushes into the mosque grunting and squealing . . . Go to Mecca and piss on the Black Stone. Overpower the Muezzin—the gee who makes the prayer call—put on a hog suit and make with the prayer call . . . Well the possibilities are unlimited.

I hereby declares the all-out massacre of everybody by everybody else. Let it Be . . . I mean we will have J-DAY once a year. All police protection suspended from the world, all frontiers open . . . No firearms. Just knives and clubs and brass knuckles and any other devices short of explosives . . .

Perhaps comes the Jihad I will have to yell "Death to the American queers!" and cut off Dave W.'s head. It's a cheap baboon trick. When a baboon is attacked by a stronger baboon, he leads an attack on a weaker baboon, and who am I to deny our glorious Simian heritage? I am working on a divine invention: a boy who disappears as soon as I come, leaving a smell of burning leaves and a sound effect of distant train whistles . . .

New character for Interzone: this international bore who comes on with "Of course the only writing worth considering is in scientific and technical journals" and reads interminable articles to his guests. Of course he concocts them himself and they mean absolutely nothing . . . Well, after a while he burns a town down, and tours the world in search of victims . . . prowling through ocean liners and hotel lobbies with his briefcase of periodicals and journals and reports from nonexistent conferences . . . I had to have one of those father-son talks with my boy this morning, you know: "Now sit down son I want to talk to you . . . Now I've had a lot of expenses lately . . . Of course I've always tried to give you every advantage . . . but it's time you took a little responsibility . . . After all I'm not made of money . . ." So he hangs his head and says, "*Tu es tan enfadado conmigo?*"—"You are so angry with me?"

Group of old queens telling each other the cute things their boy said . . . "So my boy said he could become an American because he has blond hair." "So when I tried to fuck him he said, 'Morocco for the Moroccans.'"

            Love,
              Bill

Anabasis: By St. John Perse, T. S. Eliot translation (Harcourt, Brace, N.Y., 1938).

Those Black Mountain cats: An unfortunate interrogation of Peter O. by several ex-students on the lam from Black Mt. in The Place bar, S.F. circa 1956. We complained to Bill they were intimidating Peter insistently demanding "Who are You?" . . . like "Where you at man?" The misunderstanding dissolved by the end of the decade.

Rexroth . . . attacked by juvenile delinquents: Having marital difficulties, Kenneth Rexroth complained that it was Kerouac's (or A.G.'s) fault and temporarily denounced N.Y. "beat" poets.

78.
Dec. 20, 1956
Tanger

Dear Allen,

You apparently did not receive letter I sent to to D.F. with picture of Paco, this Spanish kid wind up buggin' me like I throw him out already . . . One thing I love in the Arabs, when the job is done they put on their tents and silently steal away—unlike some Spanish citizens who want to take off their coat and throw it in a corner, stay all night and stay a little longer. What with Jack, he afraid??? When you gotta go, you gotta go and as Allah will. Maybe you better not tell him how three Arabs follow me back to my pad a few nights back and one produce a shiv at least a foot long at sight of which I am expected to swoon or cream in my dry goods . . . So I haul out my blade which opens with a series of ominous clicks, and it got six inches, Gertie . . . advance in knife fighter's crouch as illustrated inna Commando Tactics —left hand out to parry—would-be assailants take to their heels . . . They run about fifty feet and see I am not yelling copper on them—though there wasn't a copper I should yell one—so they burst out laughing and one of them comes back and mooch a dime off me which I give him at arm's length, gracious as one can be with knife in hand . . . Now I am not about to be uprooted from Tanger, and I think you will find it ideal for a place to take it cool and organize Ms. It's cheap, there are characters enough to dig, unlimited boys . . . So I suggest you stay here until early spring, when we can all make Paris—which is cold and miserable and expensive now—fuel oil shortage you know. I talk to this Spade hipster who knows everyone in the Village. I understand he used to push and now has plenty loot seems as how, well he just made Paris and say "Man it really is *nowhere* . . . " I mean when we get Ms. organized we make it . . . Morocco is really great and I know you will like it and the Arabs are not to compare with American counterparts for viciousness and it is sheer Provincialism to be afraid of them as if something special sinister and Eastern and unamerican—I met Americans in Tripoli who were afraid to venture into the Native Quarter after two years' residence . . . I went there every night . . .

The Sultan keeps exhorting his subjects to respect the lives and property of resident foreigners . . . And a military court is trying those responsible for the Meknes atrocities . . . Several death sentences so far . . . Opposed as I am to capital punishment, I cannot but feel that the practice of throwing gasoline on passersby and burning them to death should be rather firmly discouraged. Meknes has always been a trouble spot and a long way from Tangers in every sense . . . Nor would I hesitate to go there if I had a mind to or anywhere else in Morocco . . .

Garver's *ménage* sounds perfectly ghastly. If I were him I would go to England, where you can get H on RX . . . They figure an addict has a right to junk, like a diabetic to his insulin . . . Inconceivable that I should get back on junk . . .

What's with you? You wig already and remove your dry goods inna public hall??? For the Love of Jesus that cheap ham, don't bring G. If anything bugs me it's these people complaining about the sanitation . . . Such citizens should stand in Sweden. Doctor Dent is publishing an article I wrote in the January issue of *British Journal of Addiction* . . . He is one of the really great people I meet in last three years, the other being Paul Bowles . . . Don't recall I ever meet anyone I dug so quick as Bowles . . . Well he has gone to Ceylon but will return in June . . . My regards to Lucien, Jack, Peter, the whole village . . .

Porter Tuck the bullfighting hipster just passed through to N.Y. You might dig him, he will be waiter in Pablo's Spanish restaurant in East Fifties or Sixties, and will no doubt hang out in San Remo or Joe's Lunch Room, he not a junker but digs charge and friends to Stanley Gould . . . His last goring put him off the bullfight kick, he came near to die with a *cornada* in the lung . . .

I will send along about 100 pages of Interzone, it is coming so fast I can hardly get it down, and shakes me like a great black wind through the bones . . .

Of course we can all make a trip to Spain if you get tired of Tanger, which I doubt you will want to leave soon . . . Or we could dig Southern Morocco, which is great in the winter, or Portugal, which I never see . . . But I repeat, this fear of Arabs is utterly groundless . . . They are certainly much less sinister than Mexicans . . .

I can't get the Ms. organized in time to send it, and no point to send fragments—it is all like in one piece and must be dug as a continuum . . . By the time you get here it should be about half finished, though I have no way to know how long it will be, except I will know when it is done . . . Like dictation I am getting it . . . More Meknes death sentences today . . . The Istaqal say: "Order must be maintained. Cooperation with European colonists is matter of life and death for Morocco . . . We promise protection to resident foreigners. Those who leave Morocco from fear are committing a grave error." And that is the Nationalist Party speaking.

Merry Xmas, Love,
Bill

Keep me informed on sailing date. No visa needed for Tanger to date, but yes for Southern Morocco.

Garver's message: William Garver, an old connection from Times Square, occupied same building 210 Orizaba Mexico City Burroughs'd lived in 1950. Kerouac was living in a hut on the roof, writing poems (and *Tristessa*?). Peter and Lafcadio Orlovsky, Gregory and A.G. had arrived to find Garver friendly, weak and sick. He died there within a year of our departure.

What's with you? You wig already and remove your dry goods in a Public Hall???: A.G. had taken off clothes at a reading in L.A. on way to Mexico.

79.
Jan. 5, 1957
[Tanger]

Dear Allen,

I neglected to enclose the Yage photos. Those might be of value in selling the article to *True* or *Argosy*. It has also occurred to me that conceivably some grant or foundation might be interested in financing a thorough study of the subject. If so, the article and photos show what I have found out and what remains to be done. Certainly Rhine should make ESP experiments with Yage. The other plant used to prepare Yage is a very important discovery; so far as I know, I am the first to definitely identify that plant. Without it the full effect of Yage is not obtained.

Well I must get on with Interzone.

Love,
Bill

P.S. Funny how some photos seem to project the presence of the person as though his spirit resided in the picture, whereas others are just dead representation. It has nothing to do with clearness or accuracy of detail. It's more like the photo had caught and enclosed an intensity of being. Looking through my photos to find the Yage picture, I came across that picture of you where your face is divided in half by light, so that the left side of the face is in light and the right side (which is the unconscious, unknown side. Did you know that smile on the right side is a sign of violence and dangerous proclivities in the insane, whereas those who smile on the left are always tractable? A Lesbian once said of me that the right side of my face is vicious and the left side innocent) is in darkness. The picture conveys an impression of enigmatic, sinister sweetness. It always gives me a little shock when I come on it suddenly. I feel the immediate impact of your presence as if I could walk across the room and sit down on the arm of the chair in the photo.

Well, without more ado I enclose some Yage photos. In two envelopes. They might be of use in selling article to an adventure true magazine like *Argosy*, if it comes to that.

(Where or when taken on back of photos.)

80.
The dollar is going up like a beeyutiful bird.
Jan 14, 1957
[Tanger]

Dear Allen,

What's with mailing date? Interzone 150 pages, all new, comes like dictation—I hardly get time out to eat and fuck . . . Tanger is the place in the world today where the dream breaks through . . . I am trying this morning to recall details of dream where you appear in red robe . . . Instead I see equally dreamlike dream scene of actual last night . . . beautiful Arab boy lying on couch in side room of the restaurant . . . I am drinking cognac with two English queers, the boy opens his fly and pulls out perfectly formed medium-size hard cock, and I pat him on the ass and say "Another time . . . " I had two boys that afternoon come to my room, and I am about to throw them out they interrupt the Great Work . . . So one says let's make it—"Let's make it three ways." So Pepe fuck me, I fuck Pepe and Poco fuck me at the same time—it's great in the middle, just relax and let the man behind shove you up the front ass hole . . . So that's Africa, son . . .

Are you delayed and if so you ought not to be and shall I send Interzone Ms.? It is more obscene than Genet hands down and cocks up and no holes barred . . . Impossible in USA, but maybe you could get a rise out of Laughlin and I want copies scattered about, I could never reproduce it if lost my copies. Many times I don't have the slightest memory of what I wrote yesterday until I read it over, it is practically automatic writing . . . WRITE ME AT ONCE . . .

Love,

———

P.S. Situation never better in my memory . . . The Istaqal—that is, the extreme Nationalist party—says this: "Those foreigners who leave Morocco through fear are committing a grave error . . . " He refers to the French who left after Meknes riots. No one leaves Tanger . . . Nothing has happened here since one Swiss was killed in '52 . . . A number of the Meknes rioters have been tried and shot already . . .

The Sultan is one of the finest men in public life today . . . This is a fine country from every point of view . . .

Just blast a stick and walk out in the garden to dig the sunset—Arab boy on the roof next door singing "Old Lang Syne."

"Stay not on the order of your coming but *come at once*," as one member of an orgy say to another.

No Moslem or anyone else who has glimpsed the truth of God can ever again pity himself *under any circumstance.* There is *one misfortune: Not to know God.*

> 81.
> Jan. 23, 1957
> [Tanger]

Dear Allen,

Glad to hear from you at last. I will say it again and say it slow: TANGER IS AS SAFE AS ANY TOWN I EVER LIVE IN. *I* feel a chill of fear and horror at thought of the random drunken violence stalking the streets and bars and parks and subways of America. Tanger is incomparably safer than Mexico City. ARABS ARE NOT VIOLENT . . . In all my time here I know of only three people robbed—late and drunk . . . In no case did the Arabs harm them beyond taking the gelt . . . They *do not attack people for kicks or fight for kicks like Americans* . . . Riots are the accumulated, just resentment of a people subjected to outrageous brutalities by the French cops used to strew blood and death over a city block in the Southern Zone . . . There hasn't been a riot in Tanger since 1952, when one European was killed. A riot at this time is very unlikely anywhere in Morocco and above all here . . . The Sultan has shown exemplary severity in punishing the Meknes rioters and thereby serving notice that such behavior is in no way officially approved or condoned . . . So for Christ sake tell Jack to stop this nonsense . . .

Interzone is coming like dictation, I can't keep up with it. I will send along what is done so far . . . Read in any order. It makes no difference . . . My religious conversion now complete. I am neither a Moslem nor a Christian, but I owe a great debt to Islam and could never have made my connection with God ANYWHERE EXCEPT HERE . . . And I realize how much of Islam I have absorbed by osmosis without spitting a word of their appalling language. I will get to that when I, ah, have a free moment. Now hardly time out to eat and fuck . . . I have never even glimpsed peace of mind before I learn the real meaning of "It is As Allah Wills." Relax, you make it or you don't, and since realizing that, whatever I want comes to me. If I want a boy, he knocks on my door, etc. . . . I can't go into all this and all in the Ms. What's with Lucien? He need more Islam to him. We all do, and Jack especially. As one of the Meknes rioters say when they shot him: "*Skikut*"—"It is written." And remember, "God is as close to you as the vein in your neck"—Koran . . . Now I must get the Ms. in what shape I can to send . . . If you can, please have copy made and bring one with you, but leave one at least in N.Y. It would be disastrous if I lost it, as impossible to reproduce—often I do not know what I wrote last night till I read it over—the whole thing is a dream . . . Incidentally the most obscene thing I ever read. I will enclose some with this letter and send the rest separate cover. By the time you get here I expect I will have written another hundred pages supercede present material . . . Love to all and you more than anybody.

Love,
Bill

P.S. Latest is you need visa for Tanger unless they change mind again. Apply Moroccan Legation, N.Y. No doubt you *could* get in without one, but get one if possible . . . In case of fuckup at boat. (You take ferry from Gib. to Tanger, and I will meet you in Tanger.)

Address here
in case we miss at boat:
Villa Mouniria
1 Calle Magallenes
(corner Calle Cook
and Magallanes.)

82.
[No date]
[Tanger]

Dear Allen,

Must apologize for the condition of this Ms. No time to go over all of it . . . I will try to get the rest in the mail tomorrow . . . I guess you can see the idea more or less. I don't have time to revise since must keep going ahead . . . I don't know how or when I will finish, maybe just have to lop off a piece arbitrary . . . Please write when you receive Ms. and keep me inform on sailing date . . . I will meet you at the ferry here in Tanger . . . I assume you will be getting off at Gibralter, since so few passenger boats stop here . . . Be sure to check on visa with the Moroccan Consulate in New York . . .

Love to all,
Bill

83.
Jan. 28, 1957
[Tanger]

Dear Allen,

The Ms. you have seen by now—I sent it in four separate envelopes—is just preliminaries, Golden Glove kid stuff . . . Now my power's really coming and I am subject to write something downright dirty . . . I am building an orgone accumulator to rest up in and recharge myself . . . Also careful to row every day . . . A man of my caliber has to watch himself . . .

Now the latest is you don't need a visa—now you see it, now you don't . . . Well, ask at Moroccan Legation in New York if such exists, if not don't give it a thought . . . Ask around the Village if anyone knows this cat Rocky, a big spade is here in Tanger and it couldn't happen to a nicer guy. Interpol has him down as a international pusher of the white shit. We got this gossipy chief of security tells things in strictest confidence to the local Walter Winchell writes a gossip column for *The Minaret* and lives next door to me. It could only happen in Tanger. Tell Jack that Paul Bowles, who is very much afraid of violence, live twenty years in Morocco and wouldn't live anywhere else, is afraid of Mexico—where he spent a year. I really love Tanger and never feel like this about any other place. Such beauty, but more than that it's like the dream, the other dimension, is always breaking through. There is for example this square American kid here who says "I heard it was dangerous here but I never felt safer . . . Somehow I like it here better than any place." In fact we got quite a colony now, of Americans on the lam from those black tornados sweep the land of the free and suck all the meaning and beauty—the two are synonymous and no one knows what beauty is until he knows the truth of God— out of life . . . We got for example an ex-cop, an ex-school-teacher female have the affair of her life with a horrid Arab pimp disliked by everyone who know him. "Not a viler man in the Northern Zone than old Ali." And a refugee from South Africa—Johannesburg must be one of the blighted spots of the universe. And a hipster from Frisco, and Rocky, in short the town is really comes on these days . . . Alan Ansen will be here in March. Paul Bowles returns in May I think . . . Yes I know Jane Bowles.

 Now Allen, leave us have no more dilatory and come on here right away. It is important. I will meet you at the Gibraltar ferry, the Mons Culpa, and beat the fucking guides off you. They are the curse of Tanger, tell the tourists it's dangerous here to go anyplace without a guide . . . But they got this Union, it's not healthy to buck them and *The Minaret* is scared shitless to run an editorial on these foul abuses. My address here in case of fuckup at the ferry is: Hotel Mouniria, Calle Magallanes No. 1, corner Calle Cook and Magallanes.

                Love,
                  Bill

84.
31 Jan 1957
[Tanger]

Dear Allen,

This is about the last letter can reach you if you plan to leave on or about the 8th . . . I have already sent the Ms. Find I have almost complete copy here so if there is not time to have a copy made and you can leave it to advantage with someone, do so by all means. I am writing straight ahead and have another thirty, forty pages complete already . . . I mean the Ms. I sent is definitely work in progress.

Beautiful weather here . . . Incidentally I have been hitting the majoun pretty heavy of late—that is hash you take with hot tea. All the etiology of my homosex and practically everything spill right out of me . . . Quotes from last night majoun high: "So what's holding him up?—homosex orientation—Some old tired synapse won't go to its long home like it's supposed . . . there must be an answer, I need the answering service . . . I think I can arrange but it will be expensive . . . Modern Oedipus." This give me an out already, I can put down the old whore and hump some young Crete gash heat my toga like the dry goods of Nexus, you might say Nexus had the rag on . . . so the liz fuck this boy with a joke prick explode inside and blow his guts out at navel and the liz roll on the floor, laugh "Oh! Oh! Give me ribs of steel!"

And this glumph stick his proboscis up your nose while you sleep and suck out your brains, every morning you wake up with another center gone . . . A jug of paregoric and thou under the swamp cypress of East Texas . . . sweet screams of burning Nigger drift in on the warm spring wind fan our hot bodies like a Nubian slave. How obliging can you get?

The Sheriff frame every good looking boy in the County, say "Guess I'll have to hang some cunt for the new Prison," he hang this cute little corn-fed thing her tits come to attention squirt milk in the sheriff's eyes blind him like a spitting cobra . . . "Oh land's sake!" say the sheriff, "I shoulda never hang a woman. A man can only come off second best, he tangle ass holes with a gash . . . Weell, I guess I can see with my mouth from here on in Heh heh . . . " Her cunt click open like a switchblade . . . Don't offend with innocence, you need Life Boy soap, body smells of life a nasty odor stink in the nose of a decent American woman . . .

Come in at the door after the delouse treatment . . . Don't give the angel's halo lice . . .

See you soon. Look, when you get to Gib. best deal is to fly here. It don't cost much more than the ferry, less trouble with Customs and spare me the trouble of horrible scenes with the guides think I am out to steal a live one . . . weel, that's a suggestion. . . .

Love,
Bill

Feb 1

Look to see you. Don't go and die on me as the whore say to the cardiac case haw haw . . .

85.
Feb 14, 1957
[Tanger]

Dear Allen,

I was disappointed you delay. Please don't miss the Feb. 22 boat. Since sending the Ms. have written about fifty pages more, wilder than what you have . . . This is almost automatic writing. I often sit high on hash for as long as six hours typing at top speed.

I have been involved in an unfortunate affair here, gave the final fillip to my reputation. I am now known around town as of all things a nanny beater . . . It all happened like this . . . Fade out, Somerset Maugham takes the continuity . . .

"Five no trumps . . ." and other bridge table noises . . . So there they were, gathered around a bridge table in the upstairs lobby of the Hotel Cecil, as disreputable a quartet as ever spewed out the public schools of England . . . Tony G.—two forgery convictions, Colonel P.—he always leaves under a cloud before his juggled accounts stand revealed; Bob B.—old queen and Lester . . .

So the Colonel send for his money sealed in envelope, takes out some, and sends the envelope back to Bob B., manager of the hotel . . . Bob puts the envelope on a shelf behind him, meaning to return it later to the safe . . . so when he gets around to return it, it's not there . . . Now anyone at the table could have done it, and the waiter (whose nationality was never determined) subsequently fired for theft . . . The hotel denied responsibility . . . The envelope allegedly contained $500 . . .

So some weeks later I have a few drinks with the Colonel and Paul L., the English gangster, and Tony G.—he says his reputation had suffered, as if it could—so one thing leads to another:

"They can't do this to our old friend the Colonel"

"Bunch of fucking nances"

"Let's go down there and take the place apart . . . Show them what can happen if they don't pay up . . ."

"Drinks and dinner on me, boys" says the Colonel . . .

So I get in my Grade B ham actor groove and outdo everybody, they is hanging on my coattail—"For Christ sake Bill, play it cool" And me yelling across the bar "Hey, Gertie, give us another round!" Very funny, I thought, but the head of security interpreted this merry prank of middleaged cut-ups as plain extortion. The Colonel has been asked to leave Tanger—turns out he has a really bad record everyplace he goes and a notorious international heterosexual drummed out of the Tanger Country Club for pinching young girls on the ass . . . And we are all under a cloud . . . and everybody crayfishing around "I didn't mean nothing. Just had a few drinks is all." And that phony bastard Tony G. went down and got a statement from Bob B., he "just happened to be there" (It was his idea actually). And took it to the head of security . . .

The Colonel thank God is leaving day after tomorrow . . . Meanwhile he has printed up a manifesto regarding "certain unspeakable conditions obtaining in the Hotel Cecil . . . Where a huge beetle galloped across my bed not to mention the spectacle of the manager kissing the Norwegian barman in the corridors, which I personally found nauseating." And plans to give mimeographed copies to Arab street boys, distribute through the cafes of Tanger. I don't figure to be around when it happens.

I am attenuating my relations with Paul L. and company. Too much of rather a bad thing . . . And as for the Colonel: "Old man I know thee not," in words of the Immortal Bard.

Please Allen don't delay any more . . . Just as well you did not arrive a month ago, because I needed to work out my method alone. Now I am badly in need of advice, editing, collaboration. You see, Alan showed my prologue to someone in Paris. Olympia Press may be interested . . . They want to see as much as I can send in finished form but will not be able to give it attention till the beginning of April . . . It is hard for me to evaluate this material . . . Some of it should obviously be omitted and the whole put in some sort of order, but I keep writing more and no time to revise . . . I wonder how collaboration would work out . . . I think it might be terrific . . . As you see I am running more and more to prose poems and no straight narrative in over a month . . . I must take it as it comes . . . Now listen when you get here if I am not there to meet you at the dock—those Yugoslav boats subject to arrive at any hour—get in a taxi with NO GUIDE. Bastards!! Son of bitches!!—and come to HOTEL MOUNIRIA, CORNER CALLE COOK and MAGALLANES . . .

Love,
Bill

This was the last letter Bill wrote before Peter and A.G. arrived on Yugoslavian freighter at Tangier to be met at dockside by Jack and Bill. We stayed four months, worked on Burroughs' book, spent summer in Venice, travelled to Vienna and Amsterdam and settled in Paris in the fall; Bill joined us there in winter.

86.
June 15, 1957
[Tanger]

Dear Allen,

Forwarding various letters. We are now finished with the Ms., and it looks good. Alan is going back to Venice in next few days . . . Not much new around town

. . . Corpse of indeterminate nationality fished out of the bay, revolver bullet in back of head . . . The boys went back to Paris unconsummate and intact . . . At least I managed to head off Operation Milk Sugar . . . I will definitely take off at the end of this month . . . Can't drink at all . . . On the wagon . . . Feel O.K. otherwise . . . Most sinister news bulletin I ever read in the paper today: The only forms of life that mutate favorably under radiation are the smallest, namely the viruses . . . Flash . . . centipedes a hundred feet long eaten by viruses big as bed bugs under a grey sky of fallout . . .

My best to Peter . . . see you in Barcelona . . .

Love,
Bill

P.S. Addresses of queer and/or hip bars in Madrid:
Rincón Ordobez . . . . Calle Huertas
Le Panuelita . . . . Calle Jardines
Bar Tanger . . . . Calle Echegarraz
Calle Echegarraz, many other bars . .
Bar Calle Jardines . . . . *Echacaráy*
Metro Station, Plaza Mayor—for pot ask for the Fat Woman . . .

87.
July 18, 1957
London

Dear Alan [Ansen],

Went once to the Prado for half an hour . . . Spent most of my time in Madrid lying in a curtained room . . . I am definitely ill . . . Don't know the precise nature of the illness yet, pending a series of tests . . . Meanwhile can't drink even a glass of wine

. . . London is dull as ever. I have no definite plans, beyond ascertaining the nature of illness.

I wish someone would take five minutes out to send along the Ms. Leaving Word aside for the moment, and ending Ms. with Market section. After all, it takes long enough to locate a publisher without unnecessary delays. I am sending along amended version of Word cut down to thirty pages . . . But I think will split it up and scatter through the other sections . . . In any case most the rest of the Ms. can be sent out as is . . . There will always be time for additional changes . . .

It was hardly in the cards that Peggy Guggenheim should find Peter and Allen congenial . . . However, it does seem to me she is being a bit unreasonable to move in admittedly Bohemian circles and simultaneously demand conventional behavior . . .

London dull as ever of course . . . May take a trip to Copenhagen, dependent on state of health and Kells' report. He will be here in a few days . . .

                As ever,
                Bill

88.
July 18, 1957
London

Dear Allen and Peter,

Ill and bored to death as always, in London . . . Not too impressed with Spain . . . Prefer Tanger . . . I did not have impression of police state . . . In fact there is no particular control over expression, artistic or otherwise, only over overt political action . . . Spain has never been a place noted for intellectual life, and I gather there is as much going on now as there ever was . . .

I was somewhat aggrieved to learn that nothing has

been done with Ms., since God knows it takes long enough for a Ms. to circulate in any case, without purely unnecessary delays . . . After all, takes only five minutes to throw it in an envelope . . . Sending along amended version of Word, cut to thirty pages . . . I would suggest that Ms. be sent without Word, ending with Market section. No idea what I will do, depends on state of health and other factors as yet unknown . . . If I can arrange anything here on writing a book on Narcotics, will do so . . . Intend to see Elks and others working with LSD6 before I leave.

So will see you probably in Paris . . .

> As ever,
> Love . . .
> Bill

Dear Peter,
I am sure we will get along O.K. in Paris . . . See you soon.

89.
July 30, 1957
Copenhagen

Dear Alan [Ansen],

Here in Freeland. I walk in a bar and get the eye from this beautiful boy, last night being day of arrival . . . So we have a few drinks and I say something about "going back to my hotel." So he says "You mean both of us go back there?" And I say "That's the general idea." He says: "Do you want to?" And I say: "Yes" and he say: "No, I can't—" Long pause . . . "I have a wife." I don't dig it at all . . . Why does he first pin it down like that, then refuse and then lie? "Calling Doctor Benway—You are wanted in reconditioning . . ."

Sandwich bars, workman in overalls listening to classic music on the radio . . . No one talks . . . On the other hand, no one can talk longer and with less point than a Dane once you get his blood up . . .

London is by all odds the evilest place I have ever been in, a vast Kafkian maze of frustrating agencies. A Turkish Bath there beats everything anything I ever see for nightmarish horror. Like one of the more undesirable naborhoods of the Inferno, my dear . . . Incidentally nothing wrong with liver . . . It was a mild atypical hepatitis like I thought from the jump . . . So I could have spared myself that little sojourn in Hell . . . Did pick up some valuable bits of info from Dent. The LSD6 people are clamming up . . . I don't think their letters were lost. More likely not answered. They won't even talk to Dent . . . I know a trick or two would make the blighters talk soon enough . . . "You vill answer my questions now, Doctor Elk" (heavy Russian accent) . . .

Really I can hardly be expected to sympathize with your boy problems, coming from the land of fifteen-dollar tarts, and have a feeling things aren't going to be brilliant here either . . . I have not had a piece of ass since leaving Tanger . . . It's absolutely intolerable, since I refuse to masturbate . . . I don't seem to make any time without Pimp Hunger. Well I will see what can be done here and in Hamburg . . . Expect to reach Paris by October . . .

Love to all and kiss Guggenheim for me you know where . . .

Allen-Peter, sorry you are not clicking *chez* Guggenheim . . . She is strictly a Queen Bee. I thought might be worthwhile sending along copy of Ms., or at least Benway and Market, to the American agent for submit to New Directions or New Writing of something . . . See you in Paris which I hope has more innarest than what I see already.

Love,
Bill

P.S. Write cargo American Express . . . Further
research has confirmed my original impression that
Copenhagen is not the Promised Land . . . In fact
I haven't been able to do any good here to date
. . . Stuck until more money arrives . . .
Very expensive here . . . I really don't know
what the fuck I will do . . . May cut back through
Paris in another two weeks, and if that is as nowhere
as every other place I see this trip, will return to
Tanger . . . Seems to be the only place a man can
score for any ass . . . Well plans are completely
tentative . . . Two weeks is a long time and
anything can happen . . . Lots of Jazz here, which
sounds incredibly dead and tenuous, separate from
all the tension and horror that gave rise to it.

Clicking Chez Peggy Guggenheim: Peggy Guggenheim
took arbitrary dislike to Peter Orlovsky and invited A.G. to
her palazzo reception for Nicolas Calas, provided Peter didn't
come. A.G. stayed away, Calas and Caresse Crosby visited
us at Ansen's house, and everybody gossiped a bit.

90.
August – 1957
[Copenhagen]

Dear Allen,
 Received your letter related to Ms. and other matters.
I agree the best procedure is to submit personally in Paris.
However, some of the material could be sent along to the
American agent. I am not altogether clear as to the
identity or indeed existence of such a personage? Like
Benway and Market, to see what his reaction might be
and if he wants to see anymore . . . That is my only
suggestion for immediate action. Of course if you think

advisable to send any material direct to any publication or intermediary thereof, by all means do so.

My own plans in complete disarray . . . I can't seem to score for anything here . . . In fact I have seen nothing I like since leaving Tanger and am minded to return there with all possible dispatch . . . In your place I would distrust profoundly any offers tendered by G., and hesitate to meet anyone under such dubious auspices . . . I would advise apply for substantial loan to your brother, and then proceed to Paris . . . Incidentally I keep hearing about the high prices and room shortage there . . . Unless some unforeseen factors emerge—like a boy, or someone knowledgeable about LSD6, or *something* to engage my attention—I may return direct to Tanger and plan to join you later in Paris—say in mid-October . . .

I finally received a letter from Doctor Tait of Dumfries . . . I had not specifically asked him about LSD6 . . . He merely said that his dept. was not experimenting at present with *Harmaline*, but "bending their energies in a different direction . . ." How evasive can you get??

What's with Gilmore? Kells is thriving with a beautiful Danish girl and plans to spend a year here, renting house . . . I think it is not for me here, the dead level sanity and shallowness of these people appall me . . . Regards to all.

Love,
Bill

P.S. Will see what I can do about the Tanger film script . . . Nothing much so far except a documentary starting with the Chief of Security and Interpol files:

"Yes we get all kinds here in Tanger . . ." Picking up a file . . . "There was Sidi O'Leary né Samuel Greeson in Detroit Michigan . . . We knew all about him, of course . . . that is, everything about him that might interest a security officer, and there was plenty of that . . ." Thumbing through the file and reading off various offences . . . "But the story I want to tell you is not a story of crime and detection, but of a man who made a complete break with everything he had ever known and been—so complete that he lost the way back—" etc. etc. . . . Right now I am working on a straight novel involving a homosex conspiracy to take over the world. I think will model more or less on the Sodom myth, ending with atomic explosion wiping out the "Reconditioning Center" which is making queers out of everybody on assembly-line basis and the Head Interrogator finally blows it up, being as near to an arbitrary God as we can get . . . This concept has grown out of my frustration in the past month or so since leaving Tanger, and concomitant insights into certain horrible facets of the homosexual mechanism . . .

Gilmore: William Gilmore, old friend of Bill's who'd shared Brooklyn Heights house with Auden 1939 and whose sophisticated manners had made Jack Kerouac shudder with admiration.

91.
August 20, 1957
Copenhagen

Dear Allen,
I cannot see breaking with Tanger before I find something better. Since leave there have not seen anything remotely comparable from any point of view . . . And

I have learn this for sure, *I don't want to do any more traveling.* I am dead sick of living out of suitcases, shopping around in bars for dull conversation, and lousy lays at exorbitant prices. The only procedure is to pick some place, go there and stay at least three months . . . I am slowly narrowing down the earth by process of elimination . . . At least I have crossed out Scandinavia this trip, as I did Libya and whole Near East during my last bout of inconvenient, expensive and totally unrewarding travel . . .

However I cannot say that present trip has been lost on a connoisseur of horror . . . Scandinavia exceeds my most ghastly imaginations. Freeland in the Benway section was underdrawn . . . Curious that I should have known without ever having been here that the place is a series of bars along a canal . . . You did not see that section which I later dropped . . . And the R.C. is actually running full blast here, grinding out every variety of dull lunatic and not a few IND's . . . This is the police state without police, which is scene of my latest opus of which will soon send along the first chapter. Danes are at once bone dull and completely insane . . .

Most important omission in Benway section as I check over it: Page 14, sixteen lines down—"I noticed that all my homosexual patients manifested strong unconscious heterosex drives." Now *this* sentence has been omitted, which is whole point and basis of Benway's subsequent experiments in the deliberate induction of homosexuality in healthy subjects: "And all my heterosexual patients manifested strong unconscious homosex tendencies."

About plans . . . Like I say, do not feel like a trek across Europe at great personal expense to Vienna. *Not* particularly cheap, very crowded in the summer and boys very much an unknown quantity. DON'T GO TO ISTANBUL . . . I have it from those who have been there, *nowhere.* Expensive, much police surveillance—they don't like foreigners, you need a permit for everything . . . No ass, he or she . . . Incidentally the whole fucking town is in condition of rebuilding, vibrating with air hammers, bulldozers popping out all over, wreckers uncovering fixing junkies etc. . . . A nightmare I tell you . . . And if there is any place in Europe that does not welcome Bohemian visitors, this is it . . . You have been warned . . . Now Athens is possible. Cheap at least, and I think well stocked with boys. You might want to settle there, instead of Paris. I hear on all sides hair-raising stories of the Paris prices . . . no rooms, etc . . . You might find it difficult to settle there . . . What seems to me indicated is this: you get settled and I will visit you later on. I have a lot of work pending that I must be settled to do. And for a cheap satisfactory place to work, I certainly do not know of any place like Tanger. My financial situation is bad. I have run over allowance, must settle down and recoup. For this, Paris is about the last place. So I would strongly advise a look at Greece . . . Life on the Greek islands is about as cheap as any place in the world . . . Perhaps you can make arrangements in Paris . . . I don't know . . . It looks like I will be leaving here in about five or six days more . . . Proceed to Paris, dig briefly, then back to Tanger . . . You could, of course, meet me there, but you would be missing Greece which I think you should see and consider as a place to settle for a while . . . Nowhere else will Peter's $50 go farther. If you are settled there—or in Paris —then I will come for a visit of a few months or even shift residence. The point is that I don't want to travel any more at this point, and want to be very sure of any move I make. I have spent enough money to no purpose and been in enough places I wanted to get out of with all possible speed . . . Let me know what you think . . .

      Love,
      Bill

92.
August 24, 1957
Copenhagen

Dear Allen,

Received your letter with sorry tidings of unnatural brother . . . Well that's the way the ball bounces . . . If you can make Paris by mid-Sept. I will endeavor to hang on here or on location . . . that is to say, Paris proper . . . I don't want to hang any crêpe, Allen, but Paris is one hell of a place for someone without funds. I mean so much competition, so many people trying to flop on someone's floor, apartments are absolutely unprocurable, the French are real bastards . . . As for myself, Paris doesn't attract me at all. Like I say, don't like the French, nor am I partial to the anachronistic Bohemianism of St. Germain des Prés . . . I mean you can dig it in the San Remo . . . But you may find it's exactly your sort of thing . . . I don't know . . .

Copenhagen is looking up a bit. I am engaged in most curious affair with young man whose face was destroyed in an accident and completely rebuilt by plastic surgery. His pre-surgery picture is as beautiful as I ever see, and he looks just like a *copy* of it . . . but no life in his face now. In fact I think he died in the accident. He won't tell me where he lives, appears and disappears at completely arbitrary and unexpected times, like 6 A.M. . . . Rarely keeps an appointment, but I seem able to conjure him up like a junk pusher . . . I have also sampled the local trade . . . Expensive, but nice . . . Actually life here is very cheap . . . Dollar for room—anything goes or comes heh heh—thirty cents for meal . . . But drinking and boys are expensive . . .

Saw Danish movie about this boy who picks up queers, then two accomplices rush in and rob them . . . The queers are represented very sympathetically, and the robbers finally apprehended by great beefy Nordic detectives . . . But the picture doesn't come off as a documentary or anything else, all the effects and shots trite stock characters etc. . . . Nowhere . . .

I get ideas for movies all the time, like a trip around the world showing every place from the special viewpoint of someone with overwhelming specific need: Junky, queer . . . You dig, getting the eye from Danish trade in leather jacket . . . "Leather Jackets" they call the juvenile delinquents here, then getting the eye from a tough young Buddhist monk in Tibet . . . Contrasts and similarities . . . Or some deal on junk . . . It would be terrific . . .

Also have this Benway homo conspiracy underway which will be a saleable, coherent novel . . . I must settle and work, and simply don't see *la vie de Bohème* in Paris . . . But I will dig it with you, serving notice now my stay there will, barring some lovely accident, be brief . . . I am really homesick for Tanger . . .

Love to all—
Love,
Bill

P.S. My boy stood me up yesterday, but I came home late and find a note he will be around today at noon . . . He is the emptiest person I have every known . . . Faint smell of decay about him, like dried excrement in a flower bed . . . In fact he is about to feature in a novelette . . . Death in Venice sort of theme you dig . . . He is death . . . Last night I dream about him—I knew this boy, a little pansy with red hair, is dead . . . and he says: "No I just saw him." And I say "I daresay you did see him . . . I know you, baby . . ." But I allow my fantasy to run away with me. He exists . . . Kells has seen him . . . I must resist the facile ghost story angle where I show his picture to someone in a bar and he says . . . "Oh yes that's Johnny . . . Killed in a car accident three years ago . . . He was a terrible cock teaser . . ." Which he is . . . Only once in two weeks . . .

[Remainder of letter missing.]

93.
August 28, 1957
Copenhagen

Dear Allen,

    I can't cover in this letter the developments of the past week except in bare outline . . . I have always felt that the Ms. to date was in a sense notes for a novel rather than the novel itself . . . This novel is now taking shape faster than I can write it down . . . I made no mistake to come here . . . Only Scandinavia could have catalyzed the Great Work, and no other place could be the background. Briefly the novel concerns addiction and an addicting virus that is passed from one person to another in sexual contacts. The virus only passes from man to man or woman to woman, which is why Benway is turning out homosexuals on assembly-line basis . . . Real theme of the novel is Desecration of the Human Image by the control addicts who are putting out the virus . . . As Lola la Chata, Mexico City pusher, said: "Selling is more of a habit than using." I can't go into more detail now, too busy . . . It's like concepts I have in larval form for years are all falling into a pattern . . . This is correlated with my experience here . . . Everytime I reach impasse, something happens to show me the way . . . Sleep with boy the other night and whole new angle comes to me in a dream . . . A Danish cock teaser gave me essential character . . .

    So plans are in a complete state of flux . . . I hesitate

to leave this source of inspiration . . . I want to see the Northern lights, and the blighted town in Sweden that produced Urjohn . . . Did you dig how much he looked like junk? The shabbiness, neglect of person, grey, invisible quality and the depression of sexuality?

On the other hand I am out of tea and want to get back to Tanger . . . and I am short of money. In brief, don't know . . . But I can't see that Paris would give me anything at this juncture . . . In Tanger is tea and cheap living and I can settle down to work . . . There is a lot of straight work to do . . . Whole sections of Word and other parts of present Ms. are to be incorporated into present work . . . This in no way changes present arrangements for seeking publishers on Ms. as is . . . This present novel will mean at least three, four, six months intensive work . . . My feeling is looking over Ms. that many parts of it are publishable as is—Benway, Market, Voices, County Clerk—but that it does not hang together as a whole . . . So it boils down to this: If I meet you in Paris next week or two, my stay there will be brief most likely . . . I am completely in the hands of Allah or whatever you want to call it . . . *Paris is the last thing I need for this work* . . . If you are going to *settle* in Paris I could join you there, after I have completed at least a first draft . . . Say around Xmas . . . So tentatively will work and dig Scandinavia next two weeks, then head back for Tanger via Paris . . . Love to meet you there but I will be *in transit.* There is also possibility I may be hung up here longer . . . I don't know, but this is the way it looks right now . . .

P.S. Doing all right with the boys but they are expensive and not the greatest as lays . . . Love to everyone . . . Please write me at once.

Love,
Bill

P.S.   I mean don't plan on my staying in Paris now . . . It's not in my line.

P.S.   I feel very definitely that the amended version of Word is preferable . . . It contains many essential changes as well as cuts . . . I think important it should be submitted with the longer version to any prospective publisher or agents . . .

P.S.   Best thing is *wire* money c/o Bland Line American Express Tanger.

INDEX

Addams, Charles 137.
Africa 11, 13, 19, 103, 106, 111, 120, 142, 173.
Against the Law 166.
Age of Anxiety 9.
Ahmed 153.
Ali 15, 16.
Amazon River 75, 136, 141.
Amsterdam 183.
Anabasis 162.
Angelo 38, 43, 44, 52, 94.
Ansen, Alan 9, 11, 12, 13, 74, 75, 82, 87, 90, 91, 92, 93, 98, 106, 115, 142, 143, 152, 178, 183, 184, 186, 188.
Argosy 172, 173.
Arts of the South Seas 120.
As Ever 10.
Athens 9, 192.
At Sunset 114.
Auca Indians 132.
Auden, W.H. 9, 84, 190.

Bangkok 94.
Barcelona 115, 149, 184.
Baudelaire 104.
Beiles, Sinclair 9, 10.
Benveniste, Albert 21.
Berbers 115.
Berle, Milton 133.
Big Table 10.
Black Mountain 163, 167, 168.
Black Mountain Review 10, 134.
Blue Men 36.
Bodenheim, Maxwell 102.
Bogota 12.
Bosch, Hieronymous 113.
Bowles, Jane 39, 114, 178.
Bowles, Paul 15, 16, 24, 25, 49, 55, 80, 101, 104, 108, 114, 155, 163, 170, 178.
Bradbury, Ray 28.

British Journal of Addiction 170.
Brubeck, Dave 75.
Buddha 157, 158.
Buddhism 48, 50, 56, 57, 58, 78, 119.
Buddhist Bible 42.
Burford, Bob 49, 55, 58, 59.
Burns, Horne 144.
Burroughs, Joan 104, 105, 107, 114.
Burroughs, Laura Lee 34.
Burroughs, Mortimer 32, 133, 145.
Burroughs, William S. 1-10, 150, 161, 171, 183.

Calas, Nicolas 188.
California 13, 57, 58.
Cambridge Review 161.
Camus, Albert 65.
Capote, Truman 55.
Capp, Al 156.
Captain, The 62.
Carr, Lucien 142, 170, 176.
Casablanca 14, 52, 142, 145, 164.
Cassady, Caroline 64.
Cassady, Neal 6, 10, 14, 23, 26, 29, 30, 31, 33, 35, 42, 46, 50, 55, 62, 64, 91, 94, 107, 114, 116, 117, 149, 153.
Cayce, Edgar 42, 48.
Céline, Louis-Ferdinand 14.
Ceylon 163, 170.
Chandler, Raymond 21.
Chiapas 6.
Chicago 83, 97.
Christ 157.
Christianity 50.
Coleridge, S.T. 2.
Colombia 13.
Columbia College 24.
Communism 53, 156.
Confessions of an English Opium Eater 3.

Confucius 158.
Copenhagen 185, 186, 188, 193.
Corso, Gregory 5, 104, 153, 170, 171.
Cowley, Malcolm 36.
Creeley, Robert 10, 134, 137.
Crosby, Caresse 188.

Dakar 24, 101.
Dean's Bar 37.
Denmark 41, 43.
Dent, Dr. 143, 144, 170, 187.
De Quincey 3.
des Iles, Viscount 114.
Desolation Angels 133.
Dharma Bums 133.
Dover Beach 95, 118.
Driving Lesson 62.
Dryden, John 115.

East (Far & Near) 94, 95, 99, 103, 104, 108, 111, 141, 191.
Ecuador 132.
Einstein, Albert 159.
Eisenhower, Dwight 2, 53, 129.
Eliot, T.S. 161.
Elvins, Kells 11, 12, 22, 34, 35, 36, 37, 40, 43, 48, 74, 150, 185, 189, 194.
Elvins, Mr. 62.
England 127, 128, 131, 133, 140, 150, 170.
Eric the Public School Man 151, 152.
Eric the Unlucky 41, 62.
Europe 14, 75, 94, 103, 106, 111, 136, 143, 149, 191.

Fink, Mike 22.
Flee the Angry Strangers 65.
Florida 68, 77, 81, 85, 95.
Ford Foundation 98, 114.
Foreign Legion 134.
France 13.
Franco, Francisco 132.
Freetown 101, 102.
French Guinea 102.

Gaddis, William 93.
Gahm-Ehes School 73.
Gallager, Charles 98, 114, 115.
Gardi 92.
Garver, William 72, 108, 117, 170.
Genet, Jean 113, 115, 173.
Gibralter 11, 13, 59, 63, 149, 176, 177, 178, 180.
Gilmore, William 189, 190.
Ginsberg, Allen 2, 26, 28, 29, 30, 31, 55, 122, 127, 133, 168, 171, 183, 185, 187, 188.
Ginsberg, Louis 30, 31.
Girodias, Maurice 9, 10.
Goddard, Dwight 42.
Goldberg, Rube 151.
Gould, Joe 102.
Gould, Stanley 81, 89, 170.
Grant, Cary 39.
Greece 48, 115, 192.
Green, Miss 53, 80, 95, 122, 146, 153.
Guggenheim, Peggy 142, 144, 185, 187, 188.

Hamburg 187.
Harvard 11, 85.
Hemingway, Ernest 56.
Her Engagement 114.
Himmler, Heinrich 156.
Hitler, Adolph 53.
Hoeniger, Bert 23, 24, 47.
Holmes, John Clellon 36.
Hong Kong 109.
Hotel Cecil 181, 182.
Howl 107, 116, 134, 153.
Huabdropoza Indians 45.
Huie, William Bradford 65.
Huxley, Aldous 63, 82.

Ignorant Armies 95, 118.
Indiscretion 114.
Interzone 10, 77, 110, 112, 115, 117, 118, 121, 122, 123, 134, 148, 152, 154, 160, 161, 164, 168, 171, 172, 173, 175.
Invisible Man 65.
Islam 79, 167, 175, 176.

Istanbul 191.
Italy 13, 74, 75, 136.

Jackson, Phyllis 48, 49.
Japan 94.
Jewish Hospital 110.
Joe's Lunch Room 170.
Joselito 152.
Journal of a Thief 113.
Junk 78.
Junkie 135, 137.
Junky 2, 10.
Jurado, Bernabe 31.

Kafka, Franz 17, 23, 39, 88, 101, 110, 127, 187.
Kerouac, Jack 5, 6, 7, 8, 9, 10, 28, 36, 48, 49, 50, 53, 54, 55, 59, 63, 68, 77, 82, 84, 90, 93, 100, 108, 109, 114, 116, 122, 124, 133, 139, 145, 149, 153, 155, 162, 164, 168, 169, 170, 171, 175, 178, 183, 190.
Key West 53.
Kiki 2, 17, 21, 34, 37, 38, 39, 42, 43, 44, 46, 47, 50, 52, 53, 54, 56, 59, 60, 71, 76, 78, 81, 82, 94, 101, 112, 115, 116, 127, 154.
Klee, Paul 113, 114.
Koran 92.

Lamantia, Phillip 122.
Lamont, Dave 114, 125, 126, 138, 142, 151, 167.
Lao Tze 158.
Laughlin, James 174.
Lawrence, D.H. 58.
Lexington (Kentucky) 95, 131.
Libya 191.
Linton, Ralph 120.
London 131, 133, 135, 136, 137, 139, 142, 143, 145, 185, 187.
Lorca, Garcia 121.
Los Angeles 72, 171.
Lowes, John Livingston 2.

MacClay, Dr. 135.
McClure, Michael 122.
Madrid 41, 43, 184.
Majorca 98.
Malcolm the Name Dripper 39.
Mann, Thomas 9.
Mar Chica 24.
Marker 6, 36.
Marseille 49.
Maugham, Somerset 181.
Mayne, Peter 114.
Mecca 119, 167.
Melilla 81.
Merchant Marine 78, 142.
Mexico 1, 12, 13, 14, 15, 16, 22, 26, 27, 33, 35, 40, 43, 53, 68, 74, 89, 94, 103, 134, 153, 161, 171, 178.
Mexico City 26, 30, 31, 38, 108, 175.
Miami 72.
Milwaukee 68.
Mohammed 158.
Morocco 50, 98, 100, 103, 114, 163, 164, 169, 170, 171, 174, 178.
Myers, J.B. 106.

Naked Lunch 2, 5, 6, 8, 9, 10, 78, 152, 153.
Naples 146.
Nazism 156.
New Directions 63, 187.
Newman, Jerry 161.
Newsweek 93.
New York 12, 13, 66, 71, 72, 73, 75, 79, 81, 82, 98, 107, 176, 177.
New Yorker 85.
Nimon 151.

Obelisk Press 152.
Ode to Walt Whitman 121.
Olympia Press 9, 183.
On the Road 6, 49.
Oran 146.
Orlovsky, Lafcadio 109, 110, 171.
Orlovsky, Peter 6, 9, 10, 94, 104, 109, 133, 155, 159, 160, 164, 168, 170, 183, 184, 185, 187, 188, 192.

Pablo's 170.
Paco 169.
Padua 144.
Palm Beach 6, 60, 66, 67, 79.
Paris 9, 49, 55, 58, 169, 183, 184, 186, 187, 188, 189, 192, 193, 194, 196, 197.
Parise, Goffredo 74.
Paris Review 59.
Partisan Review 117.
Pepe 173.
Perone, Dr. 48.
Perse, St. John 161.
Persia 108, 115.
Peru 16, 89, 93, 95.
Poco 173.
Portugal 171.
Prado 184.
Pucallpa 114.
Pull My Daisy 6.

Queer 5, 78.
Quito 12.

Rabat 98, 150, 153.
Reich, Wilhelm 49, 58, 80.
Reisel, Victor 148, 150, 157.
Rexroth, Kenneth 75, 76, 78, 84, 142, 164, 168.
Rhine, J.B. 172.
Rhyme of the Ancient Mariner 2.
Rienzi's 12.
Rio de Oro 36.
Ritchie 67, 68.
Road to Xanadu 2.
Rome 11, 12, 13.
Roosevelt, Franklin D. 9, 76, 81, 119.
Russia 149.

St. Anthony 113.
St. Louis 27.
Santé (prison) 113.
San Francisco 6, 7, 52, 55, 63, 66, 68, 71, 75, 79, 86, 113, 115, 116, 117, 168.
San Jose 6.

San Remo (bar) 12, 170, 193.
Sargasso 117, 118, 140.
Scandinavia 143, 191, 195, 196.
Schultes, Doc 85.
Seattle 133.
Selections from Lee's Letters and Journals 112, 113.
Shakespeare 8.
Siesta in Xbalba 114.
Snyder, Gary 122, 123, 133.
Socco Chico 15.
Solomon, Carl 23, 36, 66, 150.
So Proudly We Hail 11, 150.
South America 55, 85, 89, 94, 97, 99, 103, 106, 110, 111, 117, 132, 139.
Spain 136, 137, 142, 145, 147, 149, 155, 171, 185.
Stein, Gertrude 56.
Stevens, Wallace 114, 115.
Straight Hearts Delight 10.
Strophes 114.
Subterraneans 6.
Sullivan, Dr. 54.
Sweden 170.

Tait, Dr. 189.
Tangier 1, 2, 6, 7, 8, 9, 11, 12, 13, 14, 15, 21, 24, 25, 28, 41, 48, 51, 52, 54, 55, 61, 63, 66, 67, 71, 72, 73, 75, 77, 79, 81, 85, 87, 93, 95, 98, 102, 109, 111, 114, 115, 118, 119, 124, 125, 128, 135, 136, 137, 138, 140, 142, 147, 149, 150, 151, 154, 155, 160, 161, 169, 170, 171, 173, 174, 175, 176, 178, 182, 183, 185, 187, 188, 189, 190, 192, 194, 196.
The Alleys of Marrakesh 114.
The Dead Boy and the Comets 74.
The Everglades Club 73.
The Execution of Private Slovik 65.
The First Third 6.
The Green Automobile 6.
The Invisible Man 12.
The Minaret 178.
Theosophy 57.
The Parade (bar) 39.

The Penal Colony 16, 17.
The Place (bar) 168.
The Stranger 65.
The Twilight's Last Gleaming 11.
Teheran 109.
Tierra del Fuego 44, 77.
Timbuctu 20.
Time 153.
Trilling, Lionel 116, 139.
Tripoli 146, 170.
Tristessa 171.
True 172.
Tuck, Porter 89, 170.

United States 79, 94, 95, 97, 98, 104, 113, 117, 131, 139, 147, 157, 162, 174, 175.

Vedanta 57.
Venice 9, 82, 90, 93, 98, 115, 141, 142, 143, 146, 183, 194.
Vidal, Gore 13.
Vienna 183, 191
Villa Mouniria 9.
Visions of Cody 6.

Wagner, Richard 9.
Wanklyn, Chris 114.
Warcollier 104.
West Indies 53.
Whalen, Philip 10, 122, 133, 149, 150.
Williams, Tennessee 39, 55.
Winchell, Walter 151, 178.
Wisconsin 68.
Wollman, Dave 99, 108.
Wyse, Seymour 5, 137, 139, 140, 141, 143, 145.

Yage, *Yage Letters* 5, 6, 63, 80, 81, 82, 83, 84, 85, 87, 89, 93, 100, 109, 111, 114, 128, 134, 137, 163, 172, 173.
Yoga 48, 120.
Yucatan 6, 14, 25, 26, 30.
Yugoslavia 115.

0 (Zero) 15, 21.

AVAILABLE FROM FULL COURT PRESS

Collected Poems. Edwin Denby.
I Remember. Joe Brainard.
First Blues: Rags, Ballads & Harmonium Songs, 1971-74. Allen Ginsberg.
The Luis Armed Story. Tom Veitch.
Selected Plays. Frank O'Hara.
I'll Be Seeing You: Poems 1962-76. Larry Fagin.

Dabble: Poems 1966-1980. John Godfrey.
Natural Settings. Keith Cohen.
Letters to Allen Ginsberg. William Burroughs.
Last Nights of Paris. Philippe Soupault, trans. William Carlos Williams.

Rebound Series:

Where I Hang My Hat. Dick Gallup.
The Frank O'Hara Award Books:
Spring in This World of Poor Mutts. Joe Ceravolo.
Highway to the Sky. Michael Brownstein.
North. Tony Towle.
Motor Disturbance. Kenward Elmslie.
Domes. John Koethe.